The Winning Writer

Comment

The Winning Writer avoids all the rhetoric-book routine on "How to Write Correctly" and teaches the virtue of writing from what most concerns you.
—*Wallace Stegner, Stanford University*

The Winning Writer is designed to make the student examine self, think and discover—the key to all good writing. The exercises encourage students to write what they have to say.
—*Robert Canzoneri, Ohio State University*

The strength of *The Winning Writer* seems to me to be the perceptive, challenging, and provocative exercises.
—*Jack Fulbeck, California State Polytechnic University*

In *The Winning Writer*, Robin White has said some very true things and highlighted some common misconceptions engendered by writing programs.
—*Shelby Hearon, University of Illinois*

The Winning Writer is a unique work, graced by beauty, love, and insight.
—*Robert Ginsberg, The Pennsylvania State University*

The Winning Writer is a powerful and much-needed message to pass along to writers or to anyone who wants to write.
—*Carol Holder, Faculty Development Calif. State Polytechnic University*

The Winning Writer is the kind of book I want to thrust on my colleagues, saying, "You gotta read this."
—*Marilyn F. Moriarty, Hollins College*

The key things about *The Winning Writer* are White's focus on self-expression and his positive approach to all aspects of writing.
— *John Hollowell, University of California, Irvine*

The Winning Writer

Studies in the Art of Self-Expression

ROBIN WHITE

California State Polytechnic University, Pomona

Jones and Bartlett Publishers

Sudbury, Massachusetts

Boston   London   Singapore

This book is dedicated to those great teachers who inspired me:
Carl Phelps of Kodai School, Amy Weeks of Hillhouse High,
Stanley Williams of Yale, and Wallace Stegner of Stanford—
all now gone but very much alive in spirit.

Editorial, Sales, and Customer Service Offices
Jones and Bartlett Publishers
40 Tall Pine Drive
Sudbury, MA 01776
1-508-443-5000   info@jbpub.com
1-800-832-0034   http://www.jbpub.com

Jones and Bartlett Publishers International
Barb House, Barb Mews
London W67PA
U.K.

Library of Congress Cataloging-in-Publication Data
White, Robin
    The winning writer : studies in the art of self-expression / Robin White.
        p.   cm.
    Includes bibliographical references and index.
    ISBN 0-86720-511-3
    1. English language—Rhetoric.   I. Title.
PE1408.W5803   1997
808′.042—dc20   96-32614
                                                                            CIP

Credits
Acquisitions Editor: Arthur C. Bartlett and Nancy E. Bartlett
Manufacturing Manager: Dana L. Cerrito
Design: Total Concept Associates
Editorial Production Service: Total Concept Associates
Typesetting: Celestial Engineering
Cover Design: Hannus Design Associates
Printing and Binding: Malloy Lithographing
Cover Printing: Malloy Lithographing

Printed in the United States of America

00 99 98 97 96   10 9 8 7 6 5 4 3 2 1

Acknowledgments and copyrights appear at the back of the book on page 118, which constitutes an extension of the copyright page.

Contents

Chapter 3   *Perspective*   *21*

Close observation and the power of seeing events from different viewpoints

Chapter 4   *Structure*   *29*

Strategies in the effective use of the basic forms

Chapter 5   *Planning & Outlining*   *41*

Using creative organization and the "journalist's questions" to put yourself in charge of your work

Chapter 6   *Attracting Your Reader*   *49*

How to make best use of the dynamics of what you know and feel

Chapter 7   *Maintaining Interest*   *57*

How to breathe life into your writing

Preface

When Art Bartlett of Jones and Bartlett first asked me to consider writing what has come to be known as *The Winning Writer*, I prepared a discovery draft, which I then sent to my mentor, the late Wallace Stegner, whose opinion I have valued since 1956, when I was one of his Writing Fellows at Stanford University. It was his early encouragement, as well as that of my former Stanford associate on *Per/Se* magazine—Bob Canzoneri, author and professor of English at Ohio State University—that led me to proceed.

As I did so, I accumulated a debt of gratitude to many wonderful people, including:

Jack Fulbeck, compadre, kindred spirit, poet, and Professor Emeritus, Cal State Polytechnic University, Pomona, who offered welcome suggestions as well as capricious advice on how to do what, with which, and to whom;

Robert Ginsberg, Professor of Philosophy at Penn State University, who with loving care critiqued the manuscript;

And Marilyn Moriarty, Professor of English, Hollins College; Shelby Heron, best-selling novelist; John Hollowell, Campus Writing Director at The University of California, Irvine; Patricia Hartz, director of the Humanities Core Writing Program at The University of California, Irvine; and Michel Small, Division Head of Language Arts and Social Science at Shasta College.

All helped make the review process for this book so enjoyable that I felt somewhat disappointed to see it end.

Introduction

Discovering the writer in you

ARISTOTLE WAS PERHAPS THE FIRST TO NOTE THAT "THE QUALITY OF LIFE is determined by its activities," an observation with which most of us would probably agree. Indeed, it may even seem self-evident that we are all conditioned not so much by circumstance as by our actions and reactions within the circumstance, that the entire area of individual, cultural, and social well-being is inextricably part of what we choose to do or not do, why we think we can or cannot do it.

The same, in a more intimate way, applies to writing—with one significant difference: both the quality *and* the quantity of what's written are determined by the nature of writing activities. If they are tedious, we get bored; if they are overly concerned with error avoidance, we forget about idea expression; if based on negative energy, imagination may suffer; if limited to the acceptable, creativity is often proscribed. In other words, the law of cause and effect applies: inspire anxiety, and the writer chokes; inspire confidence, and the writer sings.

Obvious as this may seem, most books designed for writing programs feature instruction not likely to give rise to the stimulating activities and positive energy needed to enhance writing. Many of these books have been prepared by those who are not primarily writers. And despite the fact that all learning, in all areas of education—formal or informal—may suffer without a clear command of language, we nevertheless find a plethora of rhetorics that arise from the abstract rather than from reality, a reality in which every self-employed author needs to enjoy the struggle in order to survive, not burn out or experience the despair of "writer's block."

Coming from this reality, I empathize with those who believe that creativity cannot be taught, that enforcing the nuts and bolts of standard English is the only way to prevent the spread of functional illiteracy, or reading and writing skills below those needed to function in today's society. But having faced for several years the challenge of teaching writing at California State Polytechnic University, Scripps College, and the University of California, I am convinced that quite the opposite is true—that creativity is innate, that it is often repressed as socially unacceptable; and that it can survive such abuse, be rediscovered, stimulated, and developed through the use of positive energy, in turn improving writing in and out of the classroom.

So this book is offered to help the writer in you sing, for experience has shown us that it doesn't much matter if you are a budding Shakespeare, would-be mechanic, aspiring doctor, hopeful athlete, or student teacher, you can improve your ability to observe and think through creatively improving your ability to write. In so doing, you can also enhance your capabilities across the board, in all fields of endeavor: self-fulfillment is inherent in the process.

The Winning Writer is thus not so much a rhetoric as a book on the art of self-expression—a testament that I hope will prove useful to you in many fields, including higher education. The basics of this art are described in the following chapters. Each will show you new and exciting ways to express yourself; each will also take you through exercises designed to increase your creativity as well as your powers of observation, analysis, and persuasion.

Welcome to the challenge.

Here is a preliminary exercise to help you reconsider, review, and rethink your attitude toward writing:

1. In a paragraph, identify what is most important to you and explain why you rank it number one.
2. In a second paragraph, describe what you consider to be your personal mission or calling.
3. Now ask yourself, "Does my interest in writing reflect my sense of mission and what I consider most important?" If "yes," explain why; if "no," list the steps you could take to start believing that what you love, what fascinates you, is worth writing about.

Chapter 1

Write On

<hr>

The winning writer's basic premises, and other

ways of enhancing perception through

self-discovery

<hr>

AMONG THE NUMEROUS MESSAGE MUGS THAT I HAVE ACCUMULATED IN my kitchen, an exuberant one features two sayings: "Success is doing what you love" and "Success is loving what you do." Welcome thoughts, but perhaps they could more meaningfully be combined into one sentence, for success is born of both—especially if the activity brings joy to others and harms no one. When you think about it, isn't it even reasonable for us to ask if we can ever really succeed at anything unless we enjoy doing it?

Of course, some people may, like Scrooge, grumble that it's possible to hate doing something and still be successful at it. This assertion sounds feasible in theory, but is it plausible in reality? Could you hate sports and become a successful athlete? Could you hate medicine and be a successful doctor? hate people and be a successful minister? hate business and be successful in business? Negative attitudes work not for but against us, while positive attitudes and expectations inspire winning efforts, making things happen rather than simply letting them happen. If this is crucial to all human endeavor, we can state categorically that it is indispensable to writing and the writer.

Energy: Negative and Positive

To understand why, we need to recognize that only two key forms of energy exist—negative and positive—and that one of the cardinal laws of physics states that energy can neither be created nor destroyed. Much the same applies to people. Each of us is endowed with only so much energy. If we spend what we have on negative feelings and activities, to the point of being consumed by them, what will be left for the positive activities that generate new energy and are so essential to creativity? If we worry about error avoidance, where will we find the energy—let alone time—for idea expression?

Now, error avoidance has long been a way of teaching people how *not* to write, what *not* to do. With the implied threat of shame as a coercive tactic, it puts a grammatical stranglehold on the use of words. Idea expression, by contrast, can be defined as the variable effort made by one person to communicate something to someone else. Artistry is the creative process that evolves, often erupts, from this attempt. It is far from perfect. Even the results are not perfect. Nothing is perfect. And we, like our expressions, are all imperfect or "flawed." However, our so-called flaws—those attributes that fail to measure up to some preconceived norm or advertised image—and not our celebrated "good" points are what make us what we are: real, laughable, different from others, and therefore unique.

Not surprisingly, then, the closer you come to understanding the human state, the closer you come to realizing that we are all fundamentally a bit strange, that the concept of "normality" is a myth. Your creativity grows through recognition of this uniqueness, for your imagination is inspired by variety, not by regimentation.

The First Law: No Two People Are Alike

The first law for you as a winning writer thus holds that no two individuals are alike, that we are all made special by our idiosyncrasies. A corollary is that loving what we do and doing what we love are predicated on the positive recognition that we evolve *because* of our differences. Without these differences, we would lack the dynamics that give rise to failure; and without failure, we would have no great achievements, all of which were prefaced by some form of failure, could only occur because of the insight or discovery arising from preliminary failure.

How many failed experiments preceded the invention of the light bulb or discovery of the polio vaccine? Which one of us has not crashed on a bicycle before learning to ride? Who even learns to walk without first falling? Where is the doctor who has never lost a patient? the lawyer who has never lost a case? the athlete who has always won? the musician, artist, or actor endowed with spontaneous, unrehearsed excellence? And where is the winning writer who has not frequently been rejected? At one time, as a way of reminding myself that the road to publication was always under construction, I saved my rejection slips until I could have papered every room in our house with them. Yet many programs that teach writing as a function of error avoidance are in reality teaching fear of failure. If the focal concern is "not failing," how can you hope to succeed? to discover? to be inspired? If you are only made anxious or fearful, how can you love to write and learn to love writing?

Welcome to the winner's circle.

If I can write because I love writing and love to write, so can you. To illustrate this, I'd like you to sit back for a moment and, forgetting judgmental concepts of right, wrong, "iffy," "no-no," and the like, visualize some person, some place, some activity, or some thing that you find intensely desirable. Then see yourself enjoying the object of your desire and, in writing, describe the experience. Do it now, using as much paper as you need to encompass your enjoyment boldly and privately.

If your mind-set was indulgent rather than anxious, chances are you will have written a robust paragraph and wanted to go on, not stop—mainly because the "fail-itis" inhibitor was not there.

The Second Law: Set Clear Goals

The second law for you as a winning writer holds that any positive expectation, any rewarding personal direction, begins with setting clear, specific goals—the sort that aren't set by those afraid of failing to reach them. All accomplishments begin with goals or dreams, and great dreams are detailed, never vague. They are also oriented around what is to be gained, rather than concerned about what might be lost, should be avoided, or should not be done.

For instance, saying what you *don't* want to write is not a goal, it is merely a negative statement; and just saying that you want to write something that will be highly acclaimed or make a lot of money is too nebulous to generate creative energy. It may also be a false goal. But saying that you want to write about the challenges faced by an illegitimate, nine-year-old crippled white girl, searching for her middle-aged adoptive black parents who have disappeared under mysterious circumstances while taking her grocery shopping on an overcast summer morning in the Chelsea district of New York City—this is specific enough to attract other ideas to it.

If you also feel compelled to write the piece because you share feelings similar to the crippled girl's, you then have emotional momentum going for you, too. And to the extent that, through your heart and soul, you touch the hearts and souls of others, you approach the shrine of greatness—which may or may not win applause and make you any money, since greatness is not a function of either. Greatness is born not of fame and fortune but of doing the best you can with what involves you and makes constructive sense of where you are. Rave reviews, notoriety, and other pleasant forms of attention are largely incidental.

The Third Law: Life Is Change

The third law of the winning writer requires us to understand and accept the fact that life *is* change—ceaseless change—and that we are all challenged by changes, large and small. In turn, each of us evolves through challenge; yet often challenges are viewed as problems to be avoided rather than opportunities in disguise, opportunities to learn and grow. To visualize this, consider the following set of associations:

Life >> change

Change >> loss   *Grief*

Loss >> challenge

Challenge >> risk

Risk >> fear

If we agree with Henri Bergson, the great French philosopher who in *Creative Evolution* postulated (perhaps borrowing from Heraclitus) that the only real definition of life is change, then we need to appreciate the fact that change involves loss. Even welcome change—recovering from a disability, quitting cigarettes, moving to an exciting opportunity in a new area—involves a degree of loss, because as we go on, what we have grown used to is left behind. Loss in turn confronts us with challenge as we struggle to minimize what is given up and maximize what is gained. As each of us must be aware—at least intuitively—every loss has an attendant degree of grief: little loss, little grief; big loss, big grief. Big Grief is the most devastating emotion that we can experience. Any time we face challenge, we also face risk, with no guarantee that things will work out. Any time we face risk, we can become afraid, knowing that when we are at risk, we are often alone and in peril.

Consider the foregoing observations a short anatomy of the human spirit or state. As a writer, you can expect to deal with all aspects of that state. The closer you come to this potentially terminal reality, the closer you come to experiencing fear, the worst form of negative energy. Yet as a writer you need positive energy in order to write. The strongest form of it is love: *loving what you do, doing what you love.* This has the power to reverse all negatives back to the beginning. For what creates life, what creates everything that makes life itself worth living, is not fear but love. You can write about fearsome events, but who could write while being awash with fear? take notes in a torture chamber? First you must clear the negative environment and begin to accept the healing power of love. Love does not destroy, love does not harm others in the name of absolutes, love does not attempt to punish or purge differences. Instead, love creates, love communicates, love makes it possible to do the impossible—climb the awesome mountain, walk the Valley of the Shadow, fearing no evil. And love will help you make your words sing.

The Fourth Law: Record Significant Moments

The fourth law of the winning writer recognizes the value of recording significant moments, or impressions that strike you for some reason. Photographs tell you what you look like; the written record captures what you feel like. Each of us deals with two realities—probably more but, as the old Yiddish joke has it, "So you got three, so who counts?" One reality is what you see. You can also touch it, hear it, taste it, smell it. The other reality is imagined. It goes beyond the five conventional or recognizable senses while nevertheless using them, as well as emotions and thoughts, to create what is not yet known, is only imagined, yet is powerful enough to alter or suspend physical reality. To cite the caption on a Hebrew University poster of Einstein: "Imagination is more important than knowledge." It is also more powerful. Recording significant moments directs our thoughts to what we feel is significant about what happens. These feelings in turn govern what we think about, and psychologically—as well as socially and professionally—each of us tends to become what we most think about. We are the history of whatever we believe or feel ourselves to be. Explore life with an open, wondering mind; record your feelings; let your imagination range far beyond the "acceptable"—and thereby know the real joy of what, through creative freedom, you truly are and can become.

Time and Place

There may be other "laws," but let's just call them suggestions, since they relate to individual preferences or variables. A crucial one is choosing the best time and place to write. For some, this may be at a desk in the morning; for others, a midday session standing by the kitchen counter can work well. Still others enjoy sprawling in the bedroom at night, enveloped in a chaos of sounds from TV and stereo. And I like to write at my desk in the morning, but I record my notes while standing by the kitchen counter at night. Too, different personal realities may mandate difficult schedules—young parents, for example, may only find the time to write before their children wake up, as novelist Ann Petry did when her daughter Elizabeth was a youngster. Also, those who hold jobs need to pick moments before and after work. But whatever is best for you is what you need to identify and stick to. This "sticking to" is key, because writing is like climbing a mountain: the goal is only achieved step by step, and the great joy of meeting the challenge comes from the progressive realization of the goal. Writing may thus discipline the mind in a rewarding and comprehensive way, but to experience the reward means being involved in and with the process. All journeys begin with one step, all books with one word. Then, step by step, word by word, the seemingly impossible becomes possible, and your spirit soars.

Good and Bad Habits

The saying holds: What counts is not what we expect of life but what life expects of us. What you get is what you give. Nothing ventured, nothing gained. However, we are all vulnerable to acquiring habits that limit or restrict what we try to do. Good habits are useful (even thieves couldn't function without them), but bad habits are either unproductive or counterproductive.

One of the most common bad habits is trying to edit or revise what you're writing while you're still writing it instead of finishing the draft and then editing. Another bad habit is pushing to make the written word *unlike* the spoken. It is and will be—no matter what—but the habit of pushing is what generates awkwardnesses, jargon, and lack of clarity. Yet any time we try to change a habit, necessary though the change may be, the new way feels weird, so we revert to the old. Try clasping your hands, for example, then changing which thumb is on top and reversing the sequence of fingers—a simple shift of a simple habit, with attendant sensations of the unnatural. Even though we know that it took time for an unsuccessful habit to become established, we resist giving the new practice any time at all because the old practice is more comfortable. The only way to change the habit of editing before finishing is to keep on finishing before editing until the new habit is the one that feels good . . . and you wonder why you ever thought otherwise.

All old habits are unmade by new practices, and the most insidious old habits are those behaviors which grow from the notion that you have to be "great" before you can dare to dream the great dream, that you have to be endowed with confidence before making plans to achieve the dream. Each of us is capable of dreaming the great dream, and confidence, as well as greatness, grows from the doing, from making plans and taking steps to achieve the goal, from falling, picking oneself up, and pressing on. Creation—incredible, wonderful, awe-inspiring creation—is all around us. To receive it, we have only to open out, not shut out. Yet often what keeps us from opening out is another bad habit: the tendency to affirm self-limitations: I can't . . . I'm no good at . . . I'm scared . . . I've never known how—expressions that are not natural but learned. We are all challenged and changed, every day, in many ways. Why beat yourself, or let the past do it? The only thing that you, I, or anyone else *has* to do is die; everything else—and I mean *everything*—is optional. So while we are alive, let's do our best.

How do you want to live? The choice is yours.

The perceptions you bring to bear in making that choice will be enhanced through the self-discovery that evolves from self-expression. I have developed and tested some exercises that can strengthen this process.

Here is the first set of them.

Exercises in Self-Discovery

A. Answer the following in writing:
    1. Who or what has most influenced you? How and why?
    2. List five of your most important personal beliefs.
    3. Note one or more of your focal obsessions and at least one key, ongoing fear.
    4. What is your most important goal? What steps do you plan to take to achieve it?
    5. Now take a new piece of paper, and at the top of it write the one word that best describes your life thus far. On the rest of the page, explain why, also noting anything you wish you could change or would have done differently.

B. Write three sentences that change the words but not the meaning of this statement:

Love is inherent, while fear is learned.

See how much you can improve the way the meaning is expressed. Then create a situation—in one paragraph—that dramatizes what you've just said.

Now do the same for the following sentence:

One of the greatest pleasures is doing
what others say that you cannot do.

C. Resolve this dilemma: you are forced to choose between exposing your best friend as a cheat or being yourself falsely accused as the cheater. What would you do? Why?

D. You are going to be given a third eye, whether or not you want it. This eye will appear on any part of your body, front or back, that you choose. What part would you select? Why? How would this change the way you perceive yourself and others? How would it change the way others perceive you?

E. Describe your vision of the ideal social date. Now describe what would be your worst date. Explain why you saw one as ideal and the other as a loser. What would happen if you discovered that the ideal was terrible and the loser quietly wonderful?

F. Rewrite the following sentence as negatively as possible:

I love the way my friends always turn the difficult problems over to me.

Now rewrite the following sentence as positively as possible:

I have to put up with the worst jerk on earth—an old gas bag who never listens.

Chapter 2

Speaking Out

Separating what you really believe

from what you think you believe or think

you ought to believe

ASSUME AT THIS POINT THAT YOU ARE IN A POSITIVE MOOD, HAVE PICKED your best time and place to write, and are ready to take all challenges in stride as you start work. Now what? and so what? What do you want to say? Why and how do you want to say it? Apart from you, who cares? In other, less painful words: How exactly do you determine your *subject, purpose, method,* and *audience?*

Tall questions. In an effort to grapple with them, let's digress for a moment to Einstein, who in *Relativity: The Special and the General Theory* (1) implied that there was no such thing as a state of absolute rest, and that the distinction between past, present, and future was an illusion. To the casual observer, such pronouncements would appear to be incorrect. A careful observer might reach much the same conclusion after noting that a rock can be completely at rest, and that we do have the record of history, that yesterday can certainly be considered the past, today the present, and tomorrow the future. With that, most of us would probably agree. But while a rock may be motionless relative to the earth, the earth itself is moving in space, taking the rock with it. And as for past and future, precisely when do they begin? At midnight? midday? According to whose clock? and where? Even as we try to identify the precise moment, the present is becoming the past as the future becomes the present. For convenience, we may have points that identify motion, and demarcations that identify blocks of time, but in reality we live in a continuum of endless, restless, changing *now* in which our actions are influenced and conditioned by preceding events that, through inexorable cause and effect, anticipate impending events.

The Search for Enduring Meanings

In this flow, each of us searches for meanings that will endure, meanings that will make sense of or give shape to our lives. What, we may ask, is the purpose of honoring our parents when we often hear them dishonoring each other and bad-mouthing acquaintances? Why should we believe in virtue when those with money, power, and influence publicly preach values but privately scoff at or ignore them? Why believe in our political system when so many politicians and the people around them lie or are on the take? Why pay attention to news so lacking in integrity that it will say anything that sells? Why even go to school if the rewards are not so much for learning as for the social prestige of looking better than someone else? In short, what purpose or significance is there to the voyage between birth and death when so much of the moral fabric of society is compromised, hypocritical, or false, and the only functional law is doing whatever you can get away with?

To find that which transcends time, we must first go through the filter of attitudes, conventions, and biases impressed upon us at an early age—attitudes about God, work, family, school, money, culture, and so on. For the sake of survival, we all subscribe to certain agreements in each area. Any attempt, no matter how thoughtful, to change or challenge them can provoke a formidable reaction (as may be evident when you merely ask a liberal and a conservative to discuss politics). But consider what happened when Jesus proposed an Eleventh Commandment, or when Galileo advanced Copernican theory, or when Darwin presented *The Origin of the Species,* or when the American colonists declared that it was the right of the people to alter or abolish existing government and institute new government, or when Margaret Sanger advocated birth control, or when Susan B. Anthony fought for the right of women to vote. What they offered was a belief that differed from what others believed, and this provoked alarm, for in every sense of the word, seeing is not believing. Instead, what we believe conditions what we see. If you believe that someone is a lush, then any glass in that person's hand will be seen as gin or vodka, even though it's only water. If you believe that the English are reserved, then someone with a British accent will seem aloof, even though he or she may be a warm, compassionate human being. Doctors who believe that the people in their waiting rooms are "patients" will have difficulty perceiving them as "clients," even though the waiting people are paying the doctor and are thus in every sense of the word the doctor's customers.

Groups cherish and adhere to safe or accepted beliefs, while the writer must struggle with truth, an unfolding, uncertain process that often ventures—at great risk—into the improbable, the impossible, the imponderable, and, especially, the improper. Indeed, truth, as Heraclitus put it, "is hard to discover and hard to attain" (2). And as Jonas Salk wryly remarked (3), eventual acceptance of any new truth goes through three stages: first, people say that it's a damn lie; then they say that there may be some truth in it, but that it isn't important; and finally they say that it's true and important but that they knew it all along.

The Truth—and the Spirit of Truth

To separate what you really believe from what you think you believe, or think you ought to believe, you must recognize the fundamental unreason of swearing to tell "the truth, the *whole* truth, and nothing but the truth." The truth is never static, complete, or insular. Only facts are—and even they may be changeable or in doubt, seen from different viewpoints. For instance, it is a fact that President John F. Kennedy was assassinated, though why and how are subject to challenge, with a lot of surrounding speculation. The truth in the ringing words of his inaugural address, on the other hand, is ongoing, unfolding. Much the same can be said for Martin Luther King, Jr., whose speeches encompassed truths that go marching on despite his death. Perhaps the closest we can ever come to truth is when we think of something that quite takes our breath away, or makes us feel a bit afraid. Those are the insights that we need to write down at once and then deal with, for we are on ground sanctified by the *spirit* of truth.

In such an environment, it soon becomes apparent that what happens is not nearly as important as how we choose to react to what happens. Good things happen to bad people, and bad things happen to good people, and vice versa. At any time, anything can happen to anyone, without rhyme or reason. What counts lies not in the situation or circumstance but in what we decide to do about it. We are in fact defined by our actions, and recognition of truth usually occurs under some form of challenge, just as the meaning of something may be discovered only when we risk losing it. Major events—both good and bad—involve major changes; major changes involve major challenges; and major challenges, either internal or external, give rise to moments of truth. Finding what you have to say can thus be a risky as well as a rewarding process of discovery, yet that is what being alive is all about.

This process is greatly enhanced when we perceive current events and issues through the extraordinary prism of myths that have shaped our lives. According to Joseph Campbell (4), these myths and legends endure because they are metaphors of existence, passed on by one generation to another. Some originate from religious tradition, others from literary tradition, and some from folklore, but all deal with the conflict of good and evil, the quest for love on a course fraught with peril. The four-letter words *good* and *evil* may be difficult to define; yet the effort to do so, to relate what *is* happening to what *has* happened, gives us valuable perspective on current events. Cultural impoverishment results when people forget that although life is a gift on brief loan, what we do with it most assuredly counts, because in all moments, in everything we do, each of us has the choice: make life better, do nothing, or make it worse. This moment is the continuum of your life.

When you take a stand on *how* and *why*, you have found something meaningful to say. That is your thesis, your message, your "mission." The more specific this statement is, the better. Any time that it also puts you at risk, you have achieved the edge of vulnerability, which is crucial to the vitality of what you have to say. For example, if you argue that it should be all right to help a terminally ill person—adult or infant—die rather than just *letting* him or her die, you've taken a stand on which you can effectively demonstrate the pros and cons of the issue. But if, instead, you claim that no moral difference exists between active and passive euthanasia, except that the passive form is legal and often inhumane, you have taken a stand that is vulnerable to fierce counterattack. This risk in turn will excite your efforts to demonstrate your contention—avoid assumptions, take nothing for granted—and the excitement then carries to your audience, that is, your readers. They may or may not agree. They may even, like some of Salman Rushdie's Moslem fundamentalist detractors, decide that you yourself are no longer fit to live. What counts is the vitality of what you have to say. No one enjoys being bored, and fresh disagreements, the fresh insights so important to the evolution of thought, are fraught with peril, are rarely boring.

Style—The Way You Say It

Many have argued that the basics of style are indispensable to writing, that what you have to say comes *after* rather than before the way in which you will say it. Such a thesis has been around for awhile, but that still doesn't make it right. What, after all, is style? *Webster's Collegiate Dictionary* defines it as "a distinctive mode or manner of expression." Distinctive? According to whom? and by what criteria? A loud burp could be called a "distinctive expression." Some babies even do it with class, to the delight of parents and friends. But is that "style"?

Looking to the experts, we may note the implication in Strunk & White's *Elements of Style* (5) that style is supposed to be the sound and proper way of putting words together. George Orwell would agree (6), adding that simplicity and the elimination of jargon are essential. But what makes style "style"? What makes it possible to distinguish Virginia Woolf from Thomas Wolfe, John Steinbeck from Gertrude Stein, Eudora Welty from Toni Morrison?

A strict high school English teacher of mine once tried to impress upon me that style was all a function of "proper grammar"—that is, writing mechanics as determined by the history and conventions of past usage. Although in retrospect I am grateful for her instruction, at the time it almost brought my interest in writing to a suffocated halt. Others have contended that style is the way in which you try to bluff, faking the illusion of wisdom or profundity. I once heard a preacher try to do this by rendering the Lord's Prayer in Tamil, the language of South India, where I was born and brought up. It so happens that I know Tamil, and what I heard was a wonderfully pious gentleman counting from one to twenty . . . and doing a pretty good "spiritual" job of it, too. But is that style?

One of the best definitions of style comes from Ernest Hemingway, who said, "In stating as fully as I could how things really were, it was often very difficult, and I wrote awkwardly, and the awkwardness is what they called my style. All mistakes and awkwardnesses are easy to see, and they called it style" (7).

Mistakes and awkwardnesses. Individual flaws. Imperfections. Felicitous idiosyncrasies. The very things that make each of us unique. Style, therefore, *is* you, is what makes you *you*. You not only *have* style, you *are* style. And the closer you come to being honestly yourself, the more distinctive your style will be. In short, what you have to say and the way in which you say it are inseparable. Both are born of the process of trying to express what *you* see, what *you* think, what *you* feel, what *you* know, as best as you can and as clearly as possible . . . in your own words, in your own way, in your own voice.

For example, notice the way that Diane Ackerman talks about the sense of touch in her book, *A Natural History of the Senses* (8):

> *Touch is the oldest sense, and the most urgent. If a saber-toothed tiger is touching a paw to your shoulder, you need to know right away. Any first-time touch, or change in touch (from gentle to stinging, say), sends the brain into a flurry of activity. Any continuous low-level touch becomes background. When we touch something on purpose—our lover, the fender of a new car, the tongue of a penguin—we set in motion our complex web of touch receptors,*

making them fire by exposing them to a sensation, changing it, exposing them to another. The brain reads the firings and stop-firings like Morse code and registers **smooth, raspy, cold.**

Now compare this to the way that Annie Dillard describes a pupa turning into a moth in *Pilgrim at Tinker Creek* (9):

It emerged at last, a sodden crumple. It was a male; his long antennae were thickly plumed, as wide as his fat abdomen. His body was very thick, over an inch long, and deeply furred. A gray, furlike plush covered his head; a long, tan furlike hair hung from his wide thorax over his brown-furred, segmented abdomen. His multijointed legs, pale and powerful, were shaggy as a bear's. He stood still, but he breathed.

While each writer is fascinated with what she is writing about, and thus attentive to detail, we can distinguish one from the other by her choice of words and word sequence. Dillard is wonderfully fond of adjectives and abrupt, descriptive phrases. Ackerman, on the other hand, enjoys a varied subject–verb–object structure. Thus, if Dillard were to rewrite Ackerman's first line, it might read, "Touch, the Parthenon of senses, urgently enfolds us." And if Ackerman were to rewrite Dillard's first line, it might read, "When the pupa struggled free, it looked a lot like damp fur." Their differences, not their similarities, are what distinguish their individual styles.

We can make the same point by comparing the styles of fiction writers, from Hemingway to Faulkner, Ann Petry to Maya Angelou, and continue to see that effective style is a matter of self. Thus, expressing yourself involves finding yourself, yet finding yourself also involves forgetting or losing yourself and just starting out. That takes confidence, and confidence is never bestowed or inborn. You learn it by earning it, and you earn it by learning it—learning that "failure" is not the end but the beginning, that so-called failing is a successful demonstration of how *not* to do it, or what *won't* work. Success is an attitude—your attitude, not anyone else's. *Doing what you love, loving what you do.* Get the right attitude, and you'll be a winner. For you can be and become whatever you want to be and become. Races have been won by people in wheelchairs, impressive art painted by those with no arms, great music composed by the deaf. Fear is the worst thing that can happen to you. Only you can say, "I can't . . . I'm no good at . . . I don't have the time . . . I lack the money . . . I'm afraid . . . "

Empowering Yourself

I can tell you how good you are, friends can tell you how good you are, God can tell you how good you are, and this may nominally "empower" you, but *you* have to believe it before it becomes real. Essentially, what happens to you depends upon you. Only you, in the final analysis, can empower yourself, and that empowerment grows from how you see yourself. If you see your limitations, you become those limitations. If you see your potentials, you will rise to them. Open out to what is all around you, become who you best can be, and bear in mind that winners commit, make things happen, look to the opportunity of challenge.

But how do you see your potentials when you have developed the habit of looking at your limitations? Try telling yourself aloud, over and over, day after day until you feel it, "What I want to say is worthwhile because *I* am worthwhile." You are. I believe it. Now you believe it.

A good way to illustrate the foregoing is to cite an example called *The Choice*, which I wrote for Behavioral Research in 1964 to create the pilot for a Job Corps project entitled *Why Work?* edited by Gordon Lish. The challenge was to produce 900 words that would not only remotivate marginally literate high school dropouts but also interest other authors in contributing to the project. Eventually, it was highly successful; but as you can see, the pilot finds its message close to the heart and uses only simple, often fragmented language to reach its audience:

> *Most of his life my father worked for next to nothing. As a missionary, he didn't have much choice. He put in long hours, seven days a week, and it was all the same. The work didn't pay. Not only that, but to many people being a missionary means being some kind of nut. So there's no class to the job, either. It's all rock bottom.*
>
> *Since my father worked for nothing, I grew up in India with nothing. When I came to the States, I had empty pockets and worn-out clothes from Goodwill bags. Some people knocked me because of my clothes. Others because of what my father was. The only dates I got were with a few girls who either liked to go for walks or sit some place and talk and didn't mind that I was a stranger in many ways—knowing nothing, knowing no one, knowing no place.*
>
> *But I was told that America was the land of opportunity. That you went to work and got paid. That the harder and better you worked, the more you got paid. That if you played your cards right, you had it made and would live happily ever after.*

So I looked for work. There were supposed to be good jobs that paid. But if there were, I couldn't find them. I just took whatever I could get. For fifty cents an hour, I washed windows, mowed lawns, did odd jobs. I also worked as a busboy, a grocery clerk, and a pushcart ice-cream man. I thumbed my way across country, shovelled dung at a dairy farm, and tossed steel for a wholesaler.

I got paid, but there was never enough to show for it—no matter how hard I worked. I lived in a cellar room next to an old hairy furnace that was either too hot or too cold. There were times when I didn't eat, and one time lasted eleven days.

If there is nothing to show for what you are doing, sooner or later you have to ask, Why do it? Why not just the hell with everything? And I thought a lot about my father then—all those years, all that work, and what did it ever come to?

The work he did was in a leper colony. Most people think that leprosy is a disease that makes your fingers and toes fall off. That can happen. But mainly, leprosy does things to your face, so that you begin to change, don't look the same, and other people tell you to stay away. And there's no place to go, nothing to do except maybe beg or steal and wait for life to kill you. That's why the leper colony was started. And that's where my father worked for next to nothing.

I often wondered why. I wondered if he got some sort of kick out of doing it. He did not. Most of the time he came home dogged and not wanting to go on.

I wondered if the work made him feel important. It did not. Mostly he took guff from everyone and anyone.

I wondered if he worked for nothing because he was afraid to ask for something. He did not. He never made a thing of being brave; but in the face of an angry mob, I'd seen him stand his ground, talking calmly.

I wondered if he chased a dream, like some Hollywood hero in the movies, a guy going around with God always on his side no matter what, and all the angels singing about it. He did not. You ever get the runs for a week in 110° shade, and life just isn't sweet-smelling any more.

I wondered about a lot of things. But it was in remembering the day we left India that I found an answer. We had gotten on the train to leave, never to come back to the only place I ever knew as home. Some friends were there at the station to say goodbye—only not the lepers because the town wouldn't allow them.

The train started up, and when it got a few miles out, there were all of the people from the leper colony waiting by the tracks. They had come there to wait, in a lonely place where no one would mind, so that when the train passed they could make a noise to let my father know how they felt. And they sent up a shrill, skin-puckering wail: U-ulu-ulu-ulu ! And my old man sat still when he heard that. And he began to cry. I never saw him cry before or after. But that day the tears ran down his leather face.

Remembering that, I found out what it was all about. My old man worked for nothing—No Thing—because he worked for love. Not for some sweet-smelling love that gets preached in clean places. Not some easy make-it-in-bed kind of love that any kid can do. But tough love. Rough, tough love that can take all the knocks and come back strong for more. Love that says: It's a fact you get born. And it's a fact you die. And in between may be stinking mean. But all you've got, all anyone's got, is the choice: Make it meaner, or make it better.

In this you can see how closely related taking a stand is to discovering what you believe.

With such an awareness in mind, now try the following:

Exercises in Taking a Stand

Use imagination in all hypothetical situations. Also, be as assertive, particular, and detailed as possible.

A. Abortion   .
1. You are the close friend of an unmarried teenage girl who has been made pregnant by your brother—
    a. Do you believe that she should or should not have an abortion? WHY?
    b. Argue FOR the opposite of what you believe, using every persuasive tactic imaginable.
2. Now assume that regardless of what you had to say, your friend went ahead and had the baby, a severely misshapen, hopelessly retarded infant—
    a. Would you encourage her to save or not save her child? WHY?

      b. Argue FOR the opposite of what you believe, using every persuasive tactic possible.

B. Euthanasia
    1. Your mother is terminally ill and in great pain—
      a. Argue FOR helping her die.
      b. Argue AGAINST helping her die.
    2 Your younger sister is terminally ill and in great pain—
      a. Argue FOR helping her die.
      b. Argue AGAINST helping her die.
    3. *You* are terminally ill and in great pain—
      a. Argue FOR suicide.
      b. Argue AGAINST.
    4. Did any change in the identity of the dying person change what you believed about helping that person? WHY?

C. Adultery
    1. You are surprised to discover that the person you are having an affair with is married—
      a. Argue FOR continuing the affair.
      b. Argue AGAINST continuing it.
    2. You are the spouse of the person who is having the affair, and have been told by others what has been going on—
      c. Argue FOR sharing your spouse.
      d. Argue AGAINST sharing.
    3. Now identify your easiest argument, your hardest, your best. Explain WHY you find them so.

Passage for Study

After you read the following article (10), briefly describe what stand the writer has taken. Then identify the "edge of vulnerability" and how it relates to the writer's key points.

> *Widowers are perhaps the least visible group in the United States and, therefore, possibly the most neglected. Yet according to the latest census, they number over two million. I became one four years ago in March.*
>
> *Until that heart-stopping moment, I had no idea that any loss could be so devastating, with sources of help not readily available, let alone apparent.*

But in an effort to help myself, or at least understand why I had heart-stoppages, memory failure, nosebleeds, cold sweats, and other frightening things, I searched for information and discovered to my astonishment that although there was a great deal of literature on widows and grief-recovery in general, there was almost nothing about widowers.

I did learn, however, that university studies had discovered that the mortality rate among surviving husbands was 61% higher than normal, with the causes of death usually being heart attacks, suicide, alcoholism and accidents—in that order.

The findings also revealed that in cases where widowers were able to establish new, caring relationships, the death rate dropped to normal or lower. While it did little good to know that I was at risk, and that my life might depend upon remarriage, the investigation raised two key questions: Why? And what made men so vulnerable?

After months of an isolation so profound that I could have rewritten Robinson Crusoe, *so complete that the touch of another hand was like a balm, and saying goodby a form of death, I learned that four factors appeared to be significant.*

The first related to social expectations of me as a man and my expectations of myself. In general, our concepts of masculinity tend to equate manhood with being strong, tough, hard as rock—anything but a "sissy." I was expected to carry on as usual, despite being torn apart inside, cut in half down the middle. And I pushed myself to fulfill the expectation, although recovery from major grief requires a greater period of convalescence than recovery from major surgery.

I was totally unprepared for the death of my wife. She had meant home to me; she had meant purpose, joy, love. And I had sought to provide for her, not myself, assuming that I would die first. I had thus developed only a small circle of close friends upon whom I could lean at odd hours for emotional support—and there were limits on how much I could lean.

Second, perhaps because of these social expectations, children are less apt to perceive the needs of a surviving father than they are of a surviving mother.

I had always enjoyed a wonderfully caring relationship with my children; yet after their mother died, my troubled, seemingly odd behavior aroused their criticism, not their understanding. Although I needed their help, often pleaded for it—especially with going through my wife's things—they did not come home after the funeral.

The only way I could see them was if I traveled—and I did, nearly passing out behind the wheel. I feel certain that this would not have been the case had my wife been the survivor; and I am equally certain that my children love me.

On the one hand pushed to recover, and on the other left alone (with the children looking on any new relationship I might enter as disrespectful of their mother), I was in a bind.

Third, I faced loss of meaningful communication with others because social life had been structured around my wife.

I wanted to share my feelings with other men—including widowers—but they tended to be leery, turning the conversation to impersonal subjects, or giving me escapist literature to read. (Read! I needed contact.) And if I tried to talk meaningfully with women, well, those I knew were the wives of my men friends and were happy to offer advice on laundry detergents, furniture polish, and so forth.

I became aware that unless others had experienced spousal death, the subject was beyond their comprehension—as it once had been for me. And those who had experienced the loss generally preferred to avoid the subject, despite the imperative that feelings be vented.

Often, a wife's death can come after a long illness, during which the husband may exhaust himself for her, only then to face the enormous exhaustion of grief itself. I spent nearly three years battling for my wife's life; everything went down with her . . . including my will to live.

And fourth, with survival largely dependent upon establishing another caring relationship—in the first few years, we're told—the widower finds himself singled in a hazardous dating world, where attitudes toward commitment have changed, while expectations of men have not.

For years, I had been devoted to one woman. With her gone, I felt out of touch, out of tune, and out of the emotional energy that has to be risked in order to discover and love another as special in her own right.

Given these seemingly hopeless imponderables, it is not surprising that widowers die at an alarming rate. What is surprising is that some of us manage to survive.

The secret is love.

Chapter 3

Perspective

Close observation and the power of seeing events

from different viewpoints

WE MAY DO A LOT OF THINGS MINDLESSLY, BUT WRITING IS NOT ONE OF them. Although in conversation we can sometimes exclude logic, reason, and the laws of cause and effect—and get away with it—any attempt to do so in writing collapses because it *obviously* makes no sense. Not only are writing and thinking inseparable, thoughts themselves need to be written down first in order to gain meaning. That is what makes the product (writing) and the process (writing) intimately a part of each other. Both depend on perspective—a point of view that allows us to appraise the evidence—so that when the writer's external and internal realities unite, or in some cases collide, the combination evolves as whole communication that the reader then completes, meaning "understands."

We know that two eyes give us visual perspective, but what gives perspective to the written word? How do we make little black letters on a flat white page seem so alive that for a while they are the reader's only reality, temporarily suspending all other realities? No sure or simple rule may exist, but one effective method is to see what you're saying from various, disparate points of view. Because our brains rely on symbols to formulate and transfer thought, no two people can ever see the same thing in quite the same way. Every individual is unique, and shifting the viewpoint from one to another enhances how we think we see what we are trying to see.

Shifting Viewpoints—Some Examples

Let's use the story of Little Red Ridinghood as an example. In this story, Little Red sets out one day in her hooded cape to take a basket of goodies to Grandmother, who lives in a gloomy forest inhabited by wolves and other wild animals. We don't know why Grandmother doesn't stay with her granddaughter's parents, one of whom has to be her son or daughter; and we have no idea why this dainty child wears a red cape or why she has been sent off on a charitable mission through an evidently hazardous area. We only know that she sets out, is accosted by the Wolf, who stupidly doesn't eat her on the spot but instead checks out Grandmother, plays a cross-dressing game in the old lady's bed, and eventually manages to snack on Little Red. By this time, however, the Lone Huntsman has arrived. He does the Wolf in and saves Grandmother and granddaughter by removing them alive, we're told, from the Wolf's bowels, which apparently function like a python's.

How do you handle this information and persuade the reader that you're not trying to foist a psychotic nightmare on children? One way is to see things from Little Red's point of view: her dad's a drunkard, her mother has run off with another man, and Grandmother has been shut away and needs food and company. So off goes Little Red, who, in an effort to make her own world right, discovers that the *real* world is something else. Your message might thus suggest that if you expect to be a successful child missionary, you need to walk softly and know a big huntsman.

But what about the Wolf, the other key player? How do we see things from his point of view? There he is, just trying to make a decent living, despite people wrecking his environment (not to mention the sexist matter of considering all wolves male), when lo and behold! along comes an opportunity to talk politics across the generations, maybe persuade both old and young to join the National Wildlife Federation, join the Sierra Club, *do* something to save the forest and the environment. Unfortunately, just as the Wolf is about to succeed, a hunter shows up, convinced that all wolves are bad guys, and ruins everything. Here, your message might be that the story from Little Red's viewpoint was the beginning of a lot of bad press for timber wolves, shy canines who don't attack people.

The same basic events can also be seen from the grandmother's point of view, the huntsman's, the parents', the nearby town's, the wolf cub's, even the forest's, as well as child psychologists, social workers, news analysts, politicians, and other stage hands. To turn things around—not assume that life has only one reality—may be the surest way to discover your own internal reality, then recreate the illusion of reality that reaches the reader.

In addition to inspiring new insights, the effort to explore various points of view can also minimize the risk of unintentionally or inadvertently offending someone. For instance, if you look at the preceding paragraph as a dramatist, you may see that the relationship between actor and support personnel is a complementary one. But if you look at it from the viewpoint of a child psychologist, social worker, news analyst, or politician, you can see how being called a "stage hand" might well be annoying, since their jobs—understanding, helping, reporting, or legislating—are all ways of acting on the stage of life.

But an even more important reason to explore differing viewpoints is that writing itself is an act of faith in the unseen—faith that an evolving internal truth does exist, and that fragmented external evidence is the symptom of it. For instance, we seek the truth, believe in the truth, as if it were something singular. Yet do we even know what the truth really *is?* and can we ever find or possess it?

When giving testimony in a court of law, for instance, we are asked to tell "the truth, the whole truth, and nothing but the truth," and everyone—perjurers excepted—usually swears without hesitation to do so. But whose truth are we talking about? and what makes the difference between individual truths—those things that might be true for one but not true for another? Two people can witness the same event and give conflicting accounts of it, just as a family can experience something together and later on find that different members disagree about what happened.

The more we grapple with such imponderables, the closer we come to an awareness that whatever any one person sees is conditioned by his or her beliefs, individual beliefs which in turn derive from group belief systems. The truth thus tends to be encompassed rather than known, and the ability to encompass it evolves from perspective.

As another example, take the story of the Three Little Pigs. In this story, the Porker Brothers want to build a house in order to protect themselves from Big Bad Wolf, but they can't agree on design and building materials, so each creates his own house. Porker 1 goes for a fancy straw cottage, Porker 2 chooses an innovative stick bungalow, and Porker 3 laboriously erects an unimaginative but solid brick edifice. Why Big Bad doesn't make his move during construction we'll never know, because he approaches only after all three Porkers have settled in and then threatens to huff and puff until he blows their houses down. The straw hut is a cinch, but before Big Bad can snatch the bacon, Porker 1 manages to escape to the bungalow. This doesn't take Big Bad much doing, either, but again the hams escape, seeking refuge with Porker 3, whom they have previously ridiculed as a punctilious fat-butt. He magnanimously lets them in, thus voiding Darwin's theory of the survival of the fittest, and Big Bad in a rage huffs and puffs himself into hyperventilation, and subsequently dies of cardiac arrest.

The story is told from Porker 3's point of view, stressing the rewards of hard work and the virtue of noblesse oblige—the generous behavior incumbent upon the truly superior. To see it from any other viewpoint takes positive energy. Without it, how can someone who believes in the work ethic see that Porkers 1 and 2 couldn't afford brick because the rule of primogeniture let Porker 3 inherit all their parents' money? And how can a wolf-hater see that the wolf's wife and children might be justified in bringing suit against the Porker Brothers for failing to get a building permit and for putting up something that resulted in the wrongful death of Big Bad?

In much the same way, how readily will someone who fears aging seek to understand or help the elderly? How often do we find people from one political extreme trying to empathize with those from the other? How usual is it to see a woman who's an ardent feminist dating, say, a right tackle who thinks a woman's place is in a cheerleader's outfit? How inclined will someone opposed to abortion be to have lunch with someone who believes it's an individual matter? Or how do Biblical absolutists, who attest to the Commandment, "Thou shalt not commit adultery," justify the New Testament assertion that the mother of *God's* "only begotten" was Joseph's wife? Truth is not an establishment, place, or institution; it is a discovery process that sets the mind free. This process is the writer's commitment. It is dependent upon perspective, and perspective is inclusive, not exclusive, accepting and open, not rejecting and closed.

Can we even hope to establish positive directions with negative instruction? As coaches of athletes have early learned, you get the best out of a team when you set objectives and practice the means to achieve them, inspiring forward momentum rather than smothering incentives with shouted admonitions. Much the same applies to writing, where the individual spirit needs to open out, wonder, explore possibilities, feel inspired, not be turned away by fear, doubt, boredom, or superficial limitations. But indispensable to achieving such a positive direction is the matter of setting clear, specific writing goals and brainstorming ways to fulfill personal expectations. Even the best of ideas needs a lot of thinking in order to grow, a lot of planning in order to become successful. It is like stopping to pick up lucky pennies. No matter how small or useless a simple thought may seem, the time taken to investigate it builds positive momentum and can often lead to surprising—as well as rewarding—revelations.

Details Make the Difference

The reference to lucky pennies might suggest some hidden belief in the influence of fate, chance, luck, accident, and so forth. Not so. The events to which we are exposed can be random, but the attention we pay to them, and the way in which we choose to react, are matters of personal choice. Observing the seemingly insignificant—the "penny" details of life—

is without exception the first step to noting something that has not yet been explained by any current theory or belief. It is from this awareness, this "gift of the present," as Annie Dillard put it in *Pilgrim at Tinker Creek*, that we pose the questions that probe the limits of human knowledge. Even if these limits are not probed, paying attention to the particulars, the so-called minor details, is crucial to establishing a believable perspective. Life might be called a "conversation overheard," but the writer has to listen to hear it, listen closely in order to re-create it.

Details are telling; in the telling are details.

Note the difference between saying, "A man and his son had some trouble with a bear when they were on a backpack in the mountains," and saying (11):

> *He and the boy were alone in the high country when the bear exploded at them from the brush, and because he had to unsling the rifle, it was the dog that made the vital difference, leaping into the charge, a flash of black and white, suddenly limp and bloody, and in that same instant he had the rifle up and fired twice in close succession, the momentum of the bear carrying it forward against the impact, all arms and bared fang, so that it took him down hard, the smack of blood and saliva hot on his face, the dense musty odor of fur enveloping him. And as he struggled free of the dead weight, knowing that he and the boy had only been bruised, not hurt, he heard first the rolling echo of his rifle shots, then in the stillness saw the dog's teeth locked in the flesh of what it refused to be overwhelmed by; and seeing them like that, seeing them still defiant though disembodied, he was seized by a paroxysm of rage against the bear and began beating and tearing at it.*

Small, seemingly unimportant details are what make the difference—not a minor difference, but a major difference, a difference made possible only by close observation that draws upon the five senses.

Perspective arises from the effort to use specific, sensory detail; yet to communicate your observations to someone else, you need to understand who or what your audience is. Even effective and affective detail has to be looked at from various points of view as you search for ways to attract or involve the reader. Thus, the more you know about the people you want to reach, the better chance you have of selecting the best perspective from which to reach them. Obvious as this may seem, the news is full of stories about well-meaning communicators clashing with potential audiences because they have tried to communicate from a perspective antipathetic to their listeners. Naturally, those who want to clash are going to clash anyway, but if your goal is to think clearly and convey what you think to someone else, you have to recognize the needs of the audience. Here, a modification of the Golden Rule may apply: Speak to another as you would be spoken to, aware that the way you like to be spoken to may not be the way the other wants or likes to be spoken to.

Implied in this view—even the foundation of it—is the concept that challenge and risk are, if not inseparable, at least interdependent: one cannot exist without the other. Where there is challenge, there is risk; where there is risk, there is challenge. Any time you try to write the best you can, you are challenged to encompass the truth, and the closer you come to some new perspective on the truth, the greater the inherent risk that you may lose it, your audience, or in some instances even your life. This is not the case with so-called safe writing—that with which many people feel comfortable—or its counterpart: commercially sanctified pandering to human depravity. But propose to a flat-world society that the world is round, or advocate the value of forgiveness to those hell bent on vengeance, and you will need to tread carefully, making the challenge exciting because the risk is great . . . as is the ultimate reward.

So no matter what area or field of writing you undertake, the integrity of intent *and* attempt makes the risk worthwhile. We evolve through this challenge, and as we evolve we continue to develop our awareness that life is a function of the means, not the ends—that if we falsify the means, we have falsified life itself. Therefore, be as true as possible to life, true to yourself, true to others, and you will truly be a winning writer.

Exercises in Perspective

A. **1.** In separate columns (left and right) list:
   a. Three major events in your life
   b. Three long-term interests
2. Now draw a line between ONE event and ONE interest that seem to you especially connected or associated.
3. Write a paragraph explaining why.
4. Then explain why from the viewpoint of:
   a. Someone older than you
   b. Someone younger
   c. Someone who tends to be critical

B. **1.** Find a photograph or painting that shows a group of people—people you don't know. Give each person a name.
2. Mentally put yourself in the group and pick the one you're most likely to get along with, the one that you're least likely to get along with.

3. Write the dialogue that would take place between the three of you.

C. First summarize the plot of a movie you've seen, then describe what would happen if you changed the lead to another character, or from one actor to another.

D. Describe what your ideal mate would be like. Now write a paragraph about what that person would—realistically—think of you.

E. In your own view, what does "playing God" mean? What would it mean to a doctor? a lawyer? a minister?

Passage for Study

Read the following excerpt (12) and rewrite it, changing the point of view from first to third person, then from the father to the younger son. What happens to the episode when you do this?

In an attempt to use the summer constructively for our disabled son Checkers, we went frequently to the beach, usually with another family or two. On a Sunday in August, we were beached at Ano Nuevo. The children were playing in the surf, paddling their boards out to catch rides on the breakers, while my wife and I were bellied in the sand, enjoying the sun and talking around a driftwood fire with another couple. I am not sure why I got up and started toward the surf, which thundered over a hundred yards away, but as I did so, I saw my younger son Parker suddenly move in a way that indicated trouble. If I had not seen that move, I would have been too late, for no one else was aware that anything was wrong. I charged across the sand, realizing that Checkers was no longer in view, and as I reached the water and bulled my way out into deep, pounding surf, only Parker was visible, and his board had been knocked from him.

"Where is he?" I shouted, coming up to him as the waves broke over us.

"I don't know, I don't know," Parker screamed back. "He was too big for me to hold."

The waves belted us down again, and when we came up, Parker was crying, "Don't let him die, Dad, please don't let him die!"

For what seemed to me forever, I was unable to find Checkers. I couldn't stay under the water, where the undertow was strong, and riding onto the crest of the breakers revealed only an endless expanse of Pacific. Then as the next wall of clear, sun-green water came up, I saw Checkers' body floating face down, and I lunged and got him. I got him by the hair, holding his face up, his body in full convulsions, letting the waves take us in until I could touch bottom, realizing only then, as I tried to stand, that I had pulled all the muscles in the back of my right thigh.

Death makes a sound, if it misses you. It is not an audible sound, but it is a sound all the same, and I heard it as I heaved Checkers up onto the wet sand—a "wfft" of the grim reaper as the scythe missed, nicking only the back of my leg, leaving the metallic taste of adrenalin dry in my mouth.

Chapter 4

Structure

Strategies in the effective use

of the basic forms

SOME PEOPLE CONSIDER ANY STRUCTURE AN UNNECESSARY RESTRAINT or discipline that inhibits free thinking and creativity. But such a view overlooks the fact that the sentence itself is structured to enhance communication and avoid such awkwardnesses as the singular/plural confusion evident in this attempt to use inclusive language: "our relationship with ourself as a person" (13). Moreover, when many sentences are combined, they find best expression through some kind of coherent form, paragraph to paragraph, beginning to end. You might even say that form is to the writer as foundations are to the architect, rhythm to the composer, surface to the painter. In short, your awareness of form is indispendable to inspiration.

Structure, however, is not single or immutable, as the antiformists are wont to think. Instead, it encompasses great variety—in writing perhaps greater than in music—and anyone who can command much of it may enjoy the fluidity commonly ascribed to virtuosos. To qualify and quantify this concept, let us consider for a moment the observation from biology that the organism with the greatest repertoire of behaviors will prevail in any ecosystem because of increased ability to adapt. When we translate this to people, we find that, say, someone who is articulate, attentive, cordial, understanding, and inquisitive will experience greater success than someone who is articulate, attentive, cordial, and understanding, but not inquisitive. The more behaviors, the greater the individual's ability to change with changing circumstance—not always, just most of the time, or enough to prevail. And there's the rub. Because when someone in authority punishes us for a behavior that he or she finds unacceptable—for whatever reason—we tend to repress that behavior, *even though the behavior itself may otherwise be good, useful, and desirable.*

29

Repressing Behavior

Take questioning. Asking questions is without doubt of great importance in any field of endeavor, and questions that probe the limits of knowledge, opening up new ways of seeing things, are indispensable to the evolution of thought. But if you are in a class or a conference or other group situation, raise your hand when the person in charge calls for questions, then find your question dismissed as absurd, when will you raise your hand again? Probably not for a while. Perhaps not ever. Does that make questioning bad? No. Nevertheless, we often inhibit, trash, deny, or, as psychologists sometimes put it, "stuff" behaviors (along with attendant anger) when we are publicly ridiculed for them.

Much the same happens—only to a more painful degree—in responses to written communication. If someone damns the form or structure you elect to use because it is not the form that he or she subscribes to, what do you do with it? It has caused you pain and embarrassment, but because you can't get rid of it, you stuff it, you inhibit it. Any time that any of us represses an optional, seemingly expendable behavior, we limit the variety necessary to thrive. So recognizing useful structures is often a matter of unstuffing good behaviors that were stuffed because some negative person pressured us into stuffing them to begin with. As a winning writer, however, you keep all options open and, in so doing, are willing to try new ways as well as exhume the old . . . nonjudgmentally.

Reality—and Beyond

One strong measure of this—the hallmark of intellect, in fact—is the ability not only to perceive accepted reality but to project beyond it. *In working with structure, we are exploring the probable relationship of one thought or concept to another.* The laws of deductive and inductive reasoning, for instance, help us to probe the unknown and draw conclusions about connecting circumstances that we have not actually seen and may not ever see. Such insights then contribute to persuasive arguments, which also depend on some form of logical structure. Our command of this clear reasoning in turn enables us to detect and/or expose errors in false arguments.

Now, philosophy departments have refined courses in logic, English departments have comprehensive programs in critical thinking, and most rhetoric textbooks feature informative sections on argumentation, all of which can be quite helpful. But the winning writer is not so much concerned with formal studies of these subjects as with the effective, affective, and ethical applications of thought patterns that enhance the art of self-expression, the chemistry of written persuasion. To restate this in the form of specific questions: How do you establish and maintain your credibility? How do you create a believable impression of cause and effect? And how do you succeed in getting your point across without inviting derision or tripping yourself up in the process? The following pages are intended to set forth and clarify—in workable simplification, in practical rather than theoretical terms—some of the key considerations.

Let us take one of the standard syllogisms used to illustrate deductive reasoning:

1. All yellow cars are cabs.
2. This car is yellow.
3. Therefore, this car is a cab.

The argument or form is valid, but the major premise is not, for we know that some yellow cars are not cabs and that some cars of other colors are cabs.

The point here is not to engage in a discussion of logic but to make you aware of the physics of human behavior, aware that every formal construct can be subject to informal misuse by those with hidden agendas.

For example, suppose that Sam wants to be promoted instead of Joe. Sam argues:

1. Anyone who drinks is an alcoholic.
2. Joe drinks.
3. Therefore, Joe is an alcoholic (implication: and not fit for the job).

Under all the conditions of formal logic, the argument is "valid"; it might convince a lot of people to believe it, and might cause Joe a painful loss of status. That is how rumors work. But, as the winning writer must be aware, #1 fails to consider matters of substance and degree—anyone who drinks how much of what?—and thus is preparing the groundwork for condemnation, not persuasion.

Consider another variation:

1. Anything that enhances brain function is good.
2. Trace amounts of manganese enhance brain function.
3. Therefore, trace amounts of manganese are good.

Should we decide not to challenge the word *anything*, we can say that if #1 and #2 are true, then the conclusion must be true. But suppose we modify this argument to read as an advertisement:

1. Medical studies show that the brain needs manganese.
2. Brand X cereal provides manganese.
3. Therefore, smart people buy Brand X.

The whole argument is flawed because it draws upon the enthymeme, or understood but not stated proposition, "Smart people do what is good and therefore buy Brand X." This renders the conclusion meaningless, since *smart* has no functional relationship to what has gone before. Yet time and again we are lured by such artifice into not only buying Brand X but also recommending it to our friends.

To the extent possible, the winning writer avoids subterfuge as well as conscious efforts to deceive—no matter how attractive the incentive—and will never intentionally foist slanted conclusions on the reader, never act in an unscrupulous way or lean into the realm of propaganda.

Propaganda

At one time, the word *propaganda* meant "the organized spread of information or doctrines by a particular group." Unfortunately, Adolf Hitler gave the word a new and sinister meaning. Today, you do not find universities and other institutions having Propaganda Offices. Instead, they have News Bureaus. Propaganda has become a "bad" word because it implies the self-serving efforts of one group to use engineered information to persuade others to believe that which may be untrue but is supposedly "above question."

Let's consider a few current examples of propagandized information:

A. 1. Animal research is evil.
   2. These doctors are engaged in animal research.
   3. Therefore, these doctors are doing something evil.

This is a "valid" argument, but the major premise is held to be "above question," and so the whole thrust of the persuasion becomes a call to stop animal research. How? Kill the doctors? Shut down the research center? What happens to those who disagree, those who suggest that animal research is important?

B. 1. The Sixth Commandment prohibits killing a human.
   2. The human starts with conception.

3.   Therefore, aborting the fertilized ovum is a sin.

Again, the structure may be sound, but the claim that a zygote is the same as a baby is considered "above question," so the basic persuasion becomes: anyone who interferes with conception is a sinner. What does this ask us to do? Does it leave any room to disagree?

C.   1.   The Bible tells the truth.
     2.   The Bible says that God created the world in seven days.
     3.   Therefore, the theory of evolution is false.

Structured argument. Curious premise held to be above question. Basic persuasion: the Bible is literally true—or at least whatever parts of it support the speaker's bias.

Miscarriages of Reasoning

These are glaring illustrations. There are many more, each fostered by fear, each preaching hate, not love, ignorance, not understanding. But the more insidious miscarriages of reasoning are subtle, based on assumptions, misperceived evidence, or faulty induction. A classic example of this is Abe Lincoln's joke (14) about the farm boy who saw the maid and a hired hand exposing themselves in the hayloft and rushed back to tell his father to come quickly, that the two were about to go potty in the hay; to which the father solemnly replied, "You've made a good observation but reached the wrong conclusion."

That is what a man from Minneapolis recently did on his first visit to Las Vegas. Noting that many cars had tinted windows, he reported to friends back home that the people in Nevada used dark glass in order to conceal their identities. Good observation, wrong conclusion. Like the farm boy who did not know about sex, the man from Minneapolis was unaware that if you don't shade the interior of a parked car, the desert sun can melt unprotected vinyl or can make the steering wheel too hot to handle, the seats too hot to sit on.

Similar wrong conclusions have been reached about the people of an entire nation, such as the observation that "Finns are melancholy," followed by the conclusion "because they must need melancholy." But the more pernicious form of flawed communication has to do with insinuation. Take the line, "Bill Clinton may have pulled strings to avoid the draft." The writer has no evidence, and the reader drops the words *may have* and hears only that "Clinton pulled strings."

Other, even more sinister forms of this flaw are studies that report, say, that "Black children are more likely to be overweight than White."

Here, the reader is set up to ignore the evidence and assume "racial inferiority," not to realize that low-income Black families may be forced to rely on cheap, fat-filled foods, and may have received little advice on nutrition apart from TV commercials.

You may have heard people proclaiming that negative emotions cause cancer, because they didn't realize that negative emotions are a *symptom* of cancer. You may have heard someone in dark glasses being called "haughty," though a few questions would have revealed that the person had undergone eye surgery and needed to wear protective lenses.

Undoubtedly one of the most remarkable examples of flawed conclusion was seen when the Nixon administration decided that fighting and surviving a "limited nuclear war" was possible. That is, they reached the conclusion first and then went out—at great public expense—to find ways to prove it. The examples they came up with were only those that indicated that major evacuations were possible.

Science may proceed in this way, too, but science cannot zealously exclude evidence that might invalidate the theory. Politicians did: none of their examples involved moving more than 400,000 people, and even an evacuation of that size took hours. An ICBM can impact in less than thirty minutes from launch. Would it be possible to evacuate a city the size of New York in that time? And if so, where would over twenty million people go, assuming that they managed to escape gridlock in the city? To the Catskills? Once there, where would they eat and sleep? go to the toilet? Even the open-air toilet activities of a few people in the countryside can be both awkward and unpleasant—but twenty million? Anyway, assuming that a reasonable number did manage to survive, what would they return to when the all-clear signal was given? Who would want to live on a wasted, radioactive planet?

This exercise in unreason is but one example of how gross an argument can become if the evidence gathered to support a premise is limited to that which is considered acceptable to promoters of the premise.

Cause and Effect—A Fundamental Law

As winning writer you are, above all, involved with the evidence and its accuracy. As winning writer you also understand the law of cause and effect—a fundamental law of human behavior, if not of the universe. All reality is a function of it: if we do this, then that will be the result; or if this is the result, then that must have caused it. No attempted persuasion—however artful—can succeed if it is based on faulty cause and effect. Even that which is contrary to popular opinion will prevail if the relationship between action and reaction, event and consequence, rings true. Of course, hoaxes can last for awhile, just as valid observations can be swept aside, but eventually, according to the law of cause and effect, fakes and censors meet their just rewards. What advances the spirit of truth will endure. Life depends on it.

In making the most of reality and what happens to us because of change, we can employ several techniques or subsidiary structural methods: comparison, definition, description, and classification. Each has a great deal to do with understanding cause and effect. Comparison, for instance, can be a simple function in the process of your deciding what jeans to buy. One pair features a fashion name, the other a standard name. Both seem to be identical, but one costs $60 and the other $20. If price is the only consideration, that will *cause* you to buy the cheaper pair. If price is not the only consideration, if on the other hand you want something that advertisements say will make you feel fashionable and sexy, you may go for the $60 pair—depending on the firmness of the guarantee that the greater price will result in enhancing your attractiveness.

A more sophisticated use of comparison might involve matters like deciding what car to buy, or whether to install active or passive solar devices to save energy. How many factors go into such decisions? What effects or results are we looking for? In buying a car, why do we pick X instead of Y when both are the same color, price, and model? Perhaps the person who wrote the advertising copy could give us the answer, since the whole thrust of advertising is to communicate information that will encourage an identified audience to choose "this" over "that." As winning writer, you understand the power of such constructs and use them fairly and effectively; for in writing, a false cause or a harmful effect aborts the sense of responsibility essential to the integrity of free speech.

Definition and Description

Among the other structural forms, two related ones are definition and description. Both are vital to the shape of writing. Definition can involve attempting to convey the meaning of either a single word—say, *dyslexia*—or a phrase such as *survival of the fittest*. A dictionary definition of *dyslexia* may be brief—"impairment of reading ability"—but to convey the connotation of the word and its associations, we need to draw upon medical explanations, social attitudes, and subjective experience, or what it's like to be dyslexic. The more we encompass a word from different perspectives, the clearer will be its meaning.

This challenge becomes complex when we attempt to define social and moral ramifications of concepts like *survival of the fittest*. The Darwinian postulate has often been lifted from its biological context and restated quite simply as: brains and brawn will predominate. Many people zealously cling to this idea. But what *is* "survival?" What *is* "fit"—let alone "fittest"? When we look at history, we can readily find instances in which the fit have been annihilated and the unfit have run governments, or robbed nations blind. Almost any political campaign may lead many of us to believe that *only* the unfit get elected to public office. Thus, for animals, survival may mean eking out a marginal existence, and *fit* may imply the power to dominate; but for people, survival involves a quality of existence that is hard to define, as well as concepts of fitness that have little to do with pushing others around—physically, socially, mentally, or financially. Survival and fitness entertain manifestations of the human spirit, and at this point definition enters the realm of philosophy.

Description is more a way of illustrating something than explaining it —of, say, showing how someone sighs rather than discussing the connotation and denotation of an exhaled or inhaled sigh as opposed to a gasp. Take words like *joy* or *sorrow*. When we describe, we show rather than define what these words mean:

> *Joy:* "As she walked, she twitched her skirt with each step and clicked her tongue in a way that evoked smiles from passers-by."

> *Sorrow:* "Slowly he knelt by her grave, head bowed, shoulders drooped in total defeat."

Similarly, when we describe a room or landscape, we engage in an act of definition that is graphic but may involve a narrative structure that opens out from the single most significant detail. Is the room a prison cell? Or is it a classroom without windows? What single first impression tells us the difference?

> **The moment she turned on the light, the scarred blackboards seemed to close in on her.**

Here, the dominant image sets an emotional tone that will govern all further details necessary to complete the description.

Classification

The last—if not final—major structural concept is more the biologist's than the physicist's gift to writing: classification. Without it, Darwin could not have developed his theory of evolution or written *Origin of Species*. Without it, few of us could make sense of life or advance our thinking.

Classification involves not only a command of comparison, definition, and description, but also the ability to organize and cluster observations in order to demonstrate shared qualities and the interrelationship of differences.

Let us consider people. When we meet someone, our observations tend to identify gender, race, ethnic origin, and a host of other externals. Without conscious effort, we form a preliminary classification, which in turn assists us with secondary classifications: stability, openness, attitude, intentions, and so forth. Each of us is unique, but in order to appreciate that uniqueness and understand the shared basis of our humanity, we go through a process of classification. In some cases, it may lead us to reject someone; but in many cases, it helps us to understand others as well as ourselves.

Your mission as winning writer is to understand, to advance the cause of shared understanding, bearing in mind that . . .

Losers:	*Winners:*
let things happen	make things happen
make excuses	make commitments
fix blame	solve problems
see work as just a job	see work as more than a job
engage in put-downs	take responsibility
seek the best for self	seek the best for all
abandon grace under pressure	have grace under pressure
want an easy way out	walk tall
think that winning is the only thing	know that winning is not everything
make wishes and count on luck	set goals and make plans
hope nothing happens	expect good to happen
use negative energy	use positive energy
take credit	share credit
fear questions	seek truth

You can be a winner. Nothing can hold you back but yourself.

Exercises in Structure

A. 1. Write a paragraph describing your best idea (of any sort or nature) and explain why you think it is your best.
    2. Now write a paragraph about everything that makes it your worst.
    3. Identify what you think are your best arguments, pro and con.
    4. Comment on each through the eyes of someone who plans to steal your idea and discredit you.

B. 1. List a few concerns that you worry about. Then describe which one you think is the worst thing that could happen to you.
    2. What would happen if it were realized? What would you do about it?
    3. How would someone you dislike respond?

C. 1. Define what you believe to be the difference between a desire and a goal.
    2. Quickly list five key desires that are important to you, and number them in order of importance.
    3. Explain why desire #1 is most important and then describe what would happen if it were realized.

D. 1. Identify in order the steps you take to make a bed. Now list the steps you would take to attract a sexual partner.
    2. Which process seemed easier? Why?
    3. Which process was more interesting? Why?

E. 1. Skipping over routine activities such as eating, bathing, and sleeping, write down the five things that you would love to do every day if you could. Place no limits on yourself or what you choose.
    2. What would happen if these five activities did become part of your daily life? Why?
    3. What would happen if you met a potential sex partner who loved to do the same things? Why?
    4. What, if anything, is keeping you from doing what you love to do? Why?

Passage for Study

You are assured that although the following news report (15) contains secondhand information, the writer has accurately conveyed what was said in the speech. Identify the speaker's bias. Are there any flaws in the argument? Why? What are they?

> *One of the state's top health care administrators yesterday gave President Clinton's health care plan a slim chance for survival.*
>
> *Leonard Schaeffer, chief executive officer of Blue Cross of California, told business and community leaders at a Whittier College luncheon that Clinton's health care plan would "never" clear the Senate or House of Representatives.*
>
> *"In his State of the Union speech, Clinton warned . . . that he would veto any bill that didn't provide universal coverage," Schaeffer said. "The question is whether he'll get a bill at all."*
>
> *Schaeffer also warned that if Clinton's plan were to be adopted, California could expect to lose up to 80,000 jobs in an employer backlash to mandatory coverage.*
>
> *"The greatest impact will be in those areas where people don't have coverage now," he said. "Those small businesses that can't afford to buy into the (health care) alliances will be the ones to lose."*
>
> *Painting an ominous picture for the 250 who attended the annual $35-a-plate event, Schaeffer characterized those who would be appointed to Clinton's seven-member National Health Care Board as "the most powerful people on earth."*
>
> *"These people will not only be setting the rules but will be determining the value of health care for the nation," he said. "These seven people will be in control of how much gets spent for your care."*
>
> *Beyond the alleged elitist and legislative nightmares, Schaeffer said that mandated health care pools or alliances would create a huge new bureaucracy estimated to cost an annual $5 billion to operate.*
>
> *"Some in the administration have said they want California to have the first [mandatory] health care alliance," he said. "That alliance would manage $80 billion annually, making it the largest economic power outside Washington, D.C."*
>
> *Under Schaeffer's guidance, Blue Cross manages approximately $8.5 billion in health benefits and controls the care and eligibility of nearly 6 million Californians.*
>
> *"Unlike voluntary alliances we have now, these mandated alliances will not foster competition because they will be saddled with price controls," he said. Schaeffer also said the term "universal health care" is misleading because under Clinton's plan, undocumented workers are not eligible.*

"I guess it's universal if you don't include California, Texas or Florida," he said.

Schaeffer said health care reform will be achieved only when a bill is presented that provides less government intervention, not more government intervention.

Chapter 5

Planning & Outlining

Using creative organization and the "journalist's

questions" to put yourself in charge of your work

MAKING PLANS CAN ENHANCE THE EFFECTIVENESS AND FULFILLMENT OF almost any task or activity, from taking off on an extended backpack, to going on a picnic. Even romance is improved when matters of time, place, and circumstance have been anticipated, however hastily. While many people might contest this, arguing that thinking ahead in such matters eliminates spontaneity, how spontaneous can you be when failure to think ahead puts you on the beach just before it starts to rain? finds you sunbathing on a bed of poison ivy? leaves you in a mosquito haven without netting or repellant? How free-spirited is the picnic that takes longer to get to than the time available because no one considered holiday traffic? Far from being a kill-joy, a plan is a flexible concept that appraises the circumstances and can promote many kinds of spontaneity.

This is especially true for writing. To have some idea of where you want to go and why you want to go there is the first step toward establishing *how* you plan to get there to best advantage—both for you and for those you hope will be interested in reading what you have written.

The Journalist's Questions

The words *some idea* involve a think-through that grows from the journalistic questions: Who? What? When? Where? Why? How? And the effort to formulate answers leads to a preliminary sketch based on free association of thoughts. As the multi-talented writer Rudyard Kipling once put it (16) in a verse that I first heard as a child:

> *I had six noble serving men*
> *Who taught me all I knew;*
> *Their names were What and Where and When*
> *And How and Why and Who.*

For example, let's assume that you have decided to write an article about sex education. Even before you can start, you need to answer some questions: What *is* sex education? Who teaches it? When is it taught? Where is it taught? Why is it taught? How is it taught? It would be a good idea to extend your inquiry to some further questions: To whom is sex education taught? To what audience is your article directed?

The more in-depth the answers, the more information you will have to work with. The answer to one question in particular—Why?—is fraught with message/mission potential. *Why* indeed? Why is sex education considered necessary today, when for centuries people got along with no formal sex education whatsoever? Why do so many parents reply evasively when their children ask a simple question about sex? And why, when sex education was first introduced, did some adults applaud while others picketed the schools? Why is it that even now, in this age of AIDS, some people are vigorously *opposed* to making condoms available to high school students while others are all *for* it? *Your* answers—not someone else's—will form the basis of what you want to say. You can take either side of the issue, but all other information that you gather is meant to develop interesting support for your thesis, persuade your audience, and make your point convincingly.

I have suggested sex education as a familiar example, but for a more complex or controversial subject, consider an essay on pornography: What is pornography? Who decides its definition? When did it start? Where? Why does it provoke so much heat? And how did it come to be considered "bad"? Each of these questions poses difficulties because the answers are either ambiguous or loaded. For instance, the answer to "What is it?" may involve comparing *Tropic of Cancer* with the illustrated *Fanny Hill*, Chaucer and Boccaccio with the *Kamasutra*, or a page from *Penthouse* with the explicit backside of a Mithuna statue at the museum in an effort to determine when pornography is art, or when art is pornography. To find out *when* it started, you will have to study history, reviewing the fertility rites of early civilizations. But if you try to discover how pornography came to be considered bad, you may run into opposition from surprising sources—opposition with formidable message potential as you discover that while murder and blasphemy may rank high on the list of thou-shalt-not's, sex usually steals the show. Why? And why do we still have laws forbidding some sexual practices that have been historically common to most, if not all, enduring relationships?

Goal-Setting

Whatever answers you reach, and whatever subject you eventually choose to write about, you will need to be involved in two crucial tasks:

goal-setting and research. While I stressed the value of goal-setting in Chapter 1 (you will find a goal-setting exercise at the conclusion of this chapter), I believe that the whole matter underlies the ability of any of us to communicate effectively and creatively. Winning obviously derives from goal-setting, and happiness involves the "act of becoming" as the goal is pursued. Failing to plan may be tantamount to planning to fail, but what plans can you make or avoid in the absence of clearly defined, desirable goals worthy of being pursued? Many people not only have failed to set goals, they have little idea of what distinguishes a goal from wishful thinking. A wish is something that you hope will happen if you get lucky without taking a gamble. A goal is an objective involving risk that requires effort to achieve *because* there are obstacles ranging from the simple to the seemingly insurmountable between you and it. Obstacles are what incline people not to set goals; and most obstacles are internal, not external. If happiness is an inside job, so is defeat. To wit, how many times have you keenly wanted to pursue something but didn't because you thought you might fail, felt you didn't have enough time or money, were afraid of the challenges involved?

As winning writer, you identify your real goals, set reservations aside, refuse to express self-limitations, and positively create the plans necessary to achieve the desired goal: you want it, you think how to do it, and you go do it. Sometimes just the process of thinking about or envisioning what you want to do can lead almost involuntarily to the objective that you have in mind, as may happen when you "see" yourself going someplace by a particular route, and later on wind up going that way, even though in the interim you decided not to.

Research

The "how to do it" first involves gathering information, another way of saying "research" (and, as some wag once remarked, plagiarism is stealing from one, while research is stealing from all). In its pure sense, research is the attempt to find out what *is* known and what *isn't* known. The less that is known about something, the more potent it may be as a subject because of the human tendency to fear the unknown. To illustrate, I'll use several hypothetical examples that quite possibly could be real.

The first concerns a man whose eldest son developed epilepsy following a head injury at age eight. At the time, the late 1950s, *epilepsy* was a closet word, and the medical pronouncement cast a shroud of gloom over the young man and his wife—until he decided to research the subject and discovered that little was known about epilepsy, and that there were no non-anonymous published articles about it because of the punitive, inhumane laws extant in many states. These laws, ranging from mandatory sterilization to incarceration, were based on fear and igno-rance of brain damage. So he wrote about what he knew, and about what it felt like to know what he knew. When this was published in a major national magazine, the response was overwhelming, and significant so-cial changes were eventually realized as other people began dealing openly with the subject.

Naturally, this young father would have preferred that his son had never been injured, or that words somehow could make everything "all right" again, but that is not reality. In reality, things happen to each of us, and whenever anything significant happens, the challenge to the writer is to research it and make known the un-known. (Compare this para-graph to the Passage for Study at the end of Chapter 3.)

The second example relates to the internal devastation experienced by a middle-aged man in the aftermath of his wife's death. It was a dev-astation so profound that the physical symptoms included heart stop-pages, violent nosebleeds, memory loss, dizziness, and other unpleasant experiences that affected his job (compare to the Passage for Study, Chap-ter 2). When he could find no fellow widower or other male friend will-ing to share feelings, he began research at the library. This ended after a few minutes when the scanner revealed thousands of articles about wid-ows and only five about widowers. Four of those five were reports on one medical study which revealed that, for reasons unknown, the death rate for male survivors of long-term marriages rose to 61 percent over normal, and that the four causes of death were suicide, heart failure, fatal acci-dents, and alcoholism—in that order. But no one seemed to know why. The answer, he sensed, was that men were afraid to discuss presumed weaknesses. So he decided to share his feelings in writing. His article ap-peared in newspapers across the nation, and the agony of male grief began to be recognized.

Of course, the man would have vastly preferred that his wife were still alive, or that grief was simply a matter of shedding some tears and get-ting on with things. But that is not reality. What is reality is the challenge to find out about what happens to us, discover the areas cloaked in igno-rance, and through writing cast the light of understanding upon them.

For a final example, let's consider the case of a nineteen-year-old woman who became romantically involved with her classmate, a young man of uncertain means. Her parents were wealthy realtors; his were struggling house-cleaners. His parents were warmly approving; hers threatened to kick her out if she did not end the relationship. This was frightening and puzzling to the young woman because her parents had always been charitable to others, and active supporters of their church's missions for the underprivileged. But instead of rebelling angrily or giv-ing up in fear, she set out in search of answers. Why? Why were her oth-erwise loving parents so incensed? Her research took her into family ge-nealogy, where, after some difficulty, she found that her parents' desire to get married had been opposed for much the same reason. The story fascinated her, and she followed up on it by writing a documentary and sharing it with her parents, who, after initial silence, tearfully realized that they had treated her the way that they had once been treated.

The Writing Process

As you can see, the question *why*, and efforts to answer it, underlie the personal beginnings of all discoveries and significant achievements. But once you have researched your subject and have some idea of what you plan to do with it, the major challenge becomes organizing so that you are in charge of your work, not your work in charge of you, so that you have enough time for the challenge instead of having to cope with stress. When under pressure, you may on occasion have to sit up all night to make a deadline. Even professional writers can face moments when they have no alternative but to write nonstop over a weekend to complete a magazine assignment on time. But while some people *do* work better under pressure, and may procrastinate without it, for most of us a more creative and rewarding method is to see how much time we have and then divide the total task into the step-by-step components necessary to complete it, allowing adequate time for revision.

Such an approach is another way of understanding writing as a process, not just a product, understanding all phases of its evolution as part of that process, not just the step of trying to fill a blank page. From idea *through* revision ∴ . . . after revision, after revision . . . thought evolves along with the effort to verbalize it. To see each aspect as part of the whole is another way of identifying the task and planning how best to meet it. Those who comprehend the value of this method will also find that it can reverse even a deep-seated tendency to procrastinate. Procrastination is born of negative energy and fear of failure, often expressed by the words, "I can't," or "I don't have time," or "I'm no good at it." Such negative energy can be eliminated by the positive when you begin to slice the total task into its easily manageable parts.

In any event, sit down right now and identify each step involved in creating your project.

That's where "luck" begins.

Exercises in Planning

A. Goal-setting:
   1. Identify:
      a. Something you have wanted to do but haven't because you lacked the money

    b. Something you have wanted to do but haven't because you lacked the time

    c. Something you have wanted to do but haven't because you thought you would fail

    d. Something you have wanted to do but haven't because you were afraid of doing it

2. From these four, pick the one goal that would make you feel good and most important if you could do it now. Write three paragraphs explaining why it is important to you, how you would achieve it, and what would happen then.

B. Planning:

1. Your goal is a romantic date, but you have only $10. How would you use that $10 to achieve your goal?

2. What kind of person would you be if you were someone of the opposite sex? How would you fulfill that concept?

3. You are going to be stranded on a deserted island and have been granted the right to take one person with you. Who would that person be? (movie and TV characters excepted), and why would you take him or her?

4. On a trip to the country, you are caught in a winter storm. Icy floods have cut all roads, and blinding snow is burying your car. You are alone, you have no car phone, and your clothing is not heavy enough to keep you from freezing without the car heater. However, you have a pack of matches, a candle, a box of granola, standard emergency tools in the trunk, and five minutes to make a survival plan before the car is buried. What steps would that plan include, and why would you include them?

5. You have just won $10 million in a state lottery. The money will be paid to you in twenty annual installments, all taxable. List everything that you would plan to do with the money, explaining why.

Passages for Study

In the following (17), note the reviewer's close attention to the director's successful incorporation of a plan:

"Body Snatchers" is at least the third version of Jack Finney's classic pulp science-fiction tale of sinister pods from outer space who take over unsuspecting humans and turn them into unfeeling automatons. Director Don Siegel did the original "Invasion of the Body Snatchers" in 1956, and given that Phil Kaufman didn't even

come close to improving on it in 1978, Abel Ferrara may seem fool-hardy to try again today.

But Ferrara hasn't merely remade "Body Snatchers," he has reimagined and reinvigorated it, using the best of special-effects talent and cool directorial skill to turn out a splendidly creepy and unsettling piece of genre filmmaking that knows how to scare you and isn't afraid to try.

One of the things that Ferrara and his . . . screenwriters have done is change the emphasis from the protest against conformity that characterized the Siegel version to look at the more modern terror of paranoia, of not knowing who is going to turn on you or when the betrayal will take place.

To restrict himself within the limits of a remake of a classic may seem like an odd choice . . . but these restrictions don't negate [his] abilities, they merely focus them.

Now observe how a writer's skill with planning enhances the dramatization of planning (18):

Before it was really light he had his baits out and was drifting with the current. One bait was down forty fathoms. The second was at seventy-five and the third and fourth were down in the blue water at one hundred and one hundred and twenty-five fathoms. Each bait hung head down with the shank of the hook inside the bait fish, tied and sewed solid and all the projecting part of the hook, the curve and the point, was covered with fresh sardines. Each sardine was hooked through both eyes so that they made a half-garland on the projecting steel. There was no part of the hook that a great fish could feel which was not sweet smelling and good tasting.

Chapter 6

Attracting Your Reader

How to make best use of the dynamics

of what you know and feel

TODAY, WE ARE EXPOSED TO SO MUCH COMMUNICATION, IN THE AIR AND ON the page, that we often face having to decide what is worth the eyestrain or earstrain and what isn't. Under such circumstances, if you as a writer would like others to read what you have written, a top priority is considering ways to attract their attention—immediately and irresistibly. This means not just writing about something interesting, important though that may be. It means creating a lead that excites and surprises, subtly, not blatantly, since arresting openers arise from the simple but effective uses of power words and power sentences. These derive more from imagination and cultural literacy than they do from large, complex vocabularies. Power words and sentences have an emotional undercurrent that draws attention to what's involved, not to the manner in which it is expressed. Quite simply, you put your reader on edge through exposure to a thought or situation that is inherently arresting.

For example, let's say that you plan to write about the inability of some men to relate to their children, and you decide to open on a personal note. Your first sentence could read:

Like many men, my father frequently experienced inordinate difficulty when trying to communicate with us.

The reader will at once be aware that you are comfortable with polysyllabic words, but consider how much stronger it is to begin with:

I learned early in life that it was pointless to make allowances for my father. (19)

The line is simple and has no elaborate words. Instead, the power word *pointless* is loaded—far more so than would be *useless, ridiculous, stupid,* or *absurd*—leading us to ask, "Why?" And whenever we are curious, or otherwise moved, we read on.

To illustrate this with another example, let's consider a situation in which you wish to convey the impression that a key member of a small group has just embarrassed himself in their presence. You could open by saying:

They were often inclined to be somewhat reserved and evasive whenever some apparently inappropriate behavior had occurred.

But how much more arresting it is to say:

It was now lunch time and they were all sitting under the double green fly of the dining tent pretending that nothing had happened. (20)

The power word in this line is *pretending*. Why are these people pretending? What has happened to cause them to do so? And would the opener be as strong if you replaced *pretending* with *assuming, thinking, feigning,* or *claiming*?

As a third and final example, we will deal with a difficult moment in which you want to convey your first impressions on being taken a political prisoner of war. You could open with:

We were led into a large room in which the over-illumination seemed magnified by plaster walls.

Clear enough, but see how much stronger it is to say (21):

They pushed us into a big white room and I began to blink because the light hurt my eyes.

Here the power words are *pushed* and *hurt*, which are stronger than *thrust* and *pained*, or *forced* and *irritated*, but not as strong, perhaps (the line is translated from the French), as *shoved* and *stung*.

We could examine many other samples of effective opening lines— from William Faulkner to Thomas Heggen, Toni Morrison to Annie Dillard—and find that all use simple language to form the surface of emotions.

That is what power words and sentences are all about: arousing the reader. Several techniques are useful in creating them. One involves saying something totally outrageous, such as clustering show-off words— "The egregious pedagogue had the pejorative hubris to implement obfuscation instead of electing the Rhadamanthine course of eschewing it"—and then trying to rephrase them simply: "The pompous instructor mouthed words that no one understood." Another technique involves writing an impossible statement, such as, "The wall punched him," and then trying to rewrite it to make sense:

There were now two holes in the wall: one where his hand was still painfully caught, the other where the bullet had just missed his head.

Obviously this is not the sort of situation that you can drop or walk away from. Neither can your reader.

A third technique (see Exercise C) is to make a list of nouns selected at random—*sky, rock, moon, field,* etc.—and then a list of verbs that are associated with only a single activity or occupation, such as carpentry—*pound, saw, break, plane,* etc.—finally connecting each verb to an unlikely noun and writing a sentence for each interconnection. For example, using *moon* and *break* might lead to seeing the new moon this way: "A broken moon slivered the water."

All such approaches are primarily methods of liberating the imagination, helping us see the many different ways in which a thought, the same thought, can be expressed. My own approach is to touch upon some feeling that takes my breath away—a feeling that is directly related to the subject—and grope for the most pointed, simple words with which to express it. For instance, if you were planning to write about the son of a physician, the breath-taking thought might be the moment of unavoidable conflict:

It was on an otherwise dull Sunday morning that Dr. Reed's son Peter announced his intention to become a witch doctor.

But it can also be effective to open with something wildly hilarious or outrageous, and other writers may prefer other methods, such as starting with a sophomoric question that demands an answer:

If we don't wake up, how can we say that the sun has risen, the day begun?

Or perhaps recounting some anecdote:

I still remember the day our mathematics teacher told us that in a line a foot long, there was an infinite number of points, and a girl in the class wanted to know how that claim could be verified. When she was put down with a derisive rebuke, I learned an important lesson: there may also be an infinite number of points in an inch, or on the head of a pin, but always be careful when you ask what an insecure person can't answer.

Or highlighting or backgrounding some pertinent, interesting, or amusing aspect of the topic's history (22):

> *Not long after Peninsula University was created by an act of God and the California State Legislature—working, as usual, hand-in-hand—there began to appear in the surrounding, or rather displaced, Bay Area towns of Marsh Flats and Los Monos a number of small communities that featured low rents and various inexpensive distractions, people included.*

Even leading with a pointed quote can be useful:

> *As George Bernard Shaw once remarked, "The man who writes about himself and his own time is the only man who writes about all people and about all time." (23)*

But whatever you choose to do, you still must face the challenge of using strong, simple words in a way that is either surprising or provocative, aware that no word is "good," "bad," "clean," or "dirty," that each word carries with it both meaning *and* feeling, the winning writer's tools.

The Power of Feelings

Unfortunately, for educational reasons that are not entirely clear, many of us have been taught that what we know takes precedence over what we feel, that knowledge is intellectual, and that feelings are untrustworthy. Such a hypothesis could not be further from the truth. What we feel determines the quality of what we know, as well as what we do with what we know. To illustrate, consider the example of two science teachers, both of whom are equally experienced and well informed. One loves teaching; the other frets about the time it takes away from personal activities such as writing articles for science magazines. The one who loves the task will grow in it; the one who does not faces burnout.

In a more focused or specialized sense, the same applies to what you choose to write about. If you are equally well informed on two separate subjects, and love one but feel indifferent about the other, the emotional imperative takes precedence over the intellectual. It is, of course, important that you know what you're writing about, but knowledge grows during the process of writing, and that process is immeasurably enhanced by what you feel. Our emotions drive us.

Most of us would, for instance, have difficulty imagining Hemingway writing effectively about fishing if what he really loved was roaring parties; and how could we picture Fitzgerald writing convincingly about party glitter if what he really loved was fishing? Would it be possible for Toni Morrison to write so evocatively about the aftermath of slavery in *Beloved* if her great fascination happened to be the problems of growing up in Beverly Hills? Or could we imagine Nora Ephron exuberantly discussing the subculture of breast worship when her real passion was dramatizing what it was like to be a post–Civil War Black?

We are what we feel, and what we feel is the basis for what we know.

Observation and Thought

This concept becomes clearer when we recognize the inseparability of observation and thought. The command of thought—any thought—is directly related to the power of observation, and the power of observation can be enhanced by positive feelings or diminished by negative ones. Someone who fears insects is not likely to be an accurate observer of insects, and someone who feels threatened by illness can have difficulty seeing beyond the hospital bed that the sick person is lying on. Research in child psychology has shown us that children who have lost one parent often see either themselves or the remaining parent as responsible for the loss. And we all know that jealousy has blinded many, not just Othello. But on a more complex level, someone who has been taught to fear differences may be incapable of seeing ways in which differences form the basis of social and individual dynamics. Such a person may actually see differences as evil (how long have the Croats and Serbs been hating and fighting each other?) and so reject any observation that does not agree with the emotional premise. Simplistically, as a familiar joke goes, someone motivated by greed may see a gold-painted brick, think that it's solid gold, and feel inspired to take advantage of the "fool" who is willing to part with it for $200.

To further illustrate this principle, let's imagine a situation in which three people are applying for the same job. The interviewer announces that only one question will be asked, and the applicant offering the best answer will get the job.

The first person enters the interview room, is asked, "What is 2 + 2?" and replies, " 4."

Then the second person enters, is asked, "What is 2 + 2?" and replies, "Well, it could be 4, or then again 22."

Finally, the third person enters, is asked, "What is 2 + 2?" and replies, "Two and two of what?"

Each applicant obviously can think, but which one observes more and therefore thinks more? Or is it thinks more and therefore observes more? It can be either way, for the power of observation and the power of thought are inseparable. Improving one results in improving both, as may be evidenced in the simple exercise of watching a ten-minute section of videotape with the sound turned off, then writing a detailed interpretation of what was happening and why, and then rerunning the tape with the sound on. A similar exercise (like one used by intelligence agencies to screen applicants) involves observing someone's house for 60 seconds, turning away to write down as many details as possible, followed by an interpretation of what sort of people live in the house and why they chose for their house the particulars that you observed. Repeating the process not only improves your ability to observe, it also increases your power of thought.

We can stretch such exercises in many different, interesting, and useful ways, keeping in mind that the most persuasive writing involves *showing* rather than *telling*—letting your reader *see* what's happening, *hear* what's happening, *feel* what's happening, *smell* what's happening, even *taste* what's happening. For example, supposing you are at a race track and one of the horses falls, crushing the jockey. You could *tell* the reader that you saw a terrible accident at the horse races, but how much more forceful to *show* the incident by letting the reader hear the thunder of hooves, feel the ground shake, smell the sweat, taste dust in the air, see the crowd suddenly lurch forward with a gasp as the jockey's lungs pop.

To the extent that you observe life around you, you can do this. But observation involves *all* the senses, not just sight. And whatever you perceive, even with great accuracy, is enormously improved by a sense of humor—in grim moments as well as glad. Humor is to thought as salt is to food: it adds to the flavor. Sometimes we're told that laughter is shallow, seriousness profound; but laughter and seriousness are two sides of the same coin, as Shakespeare readily demonstrated in his use of comic relief following moments of the utmost gravity. Moreover, a sense of humor is the hallmark of intelligence. Grim observers rarely get the whole picture, and bemused observers realize that *no one* gets the whole anything, let alone picture. Comic relief saves us from blindness in the most difficult of times. Indeed, if laughter is one of God's greatest gifts to humans, a sense of humor is surely one of your most formidable assets as a winning writer. So let us always remember that what is intellectual does not have to put us to sleep, that what is raucous is not necessarily bad.

Exercises in Power Attraction

A. 1. Complete the following sentence: "If I could feel what I see and think what I know, I would . . ."

2. Now pick someone you dislike and, in a paragraph, explain to him or her why what you feel, see, think, and know is interesting.

B. Write the words *love* and *fear,* and under each write the word that comes to mind when you think what each:
1. Smells like
2. Feels like
3. Tastes like
4. Looks like
5. Sounds like
Use these words in two paragraphs, one that conveys love, and one that conveys fear, but do not use the words *love* or *fear.*

C. 1. In one column, write five random nouns; in the next write five verbs related to only one activity.
2. Take what you consider the most absurd word from one column, connect it to the most absurd word from the second column, and write a sentence that uses both.
3. Work a revised version of this sentence to open your paragraph on love. Then select the next most absurd words from your lists, create a sentence from them, and adapt it to open your paragraph on fear.

D. Watch someone you do not know for five minutes, and write an interpretation of what that person was doing. Also include in your interpretation the dominant clue from each of the five senses: sight, sound, smell, touch, taste.

Passages for Study

In the following openings from three books—highly successful but quite different in subject, point of view, and direction—identify the elements that make you want to read on, and explain why they do. Is any one opening stronger that the others? If so, why? Could you improve it?

124 was spiteful. Full of baby's venom. The women in the house knew it and so did the children. For years each put up with the spite in his own way, but by 1873 Sethe and her daughter Denver were its only victims. The grandmother, Baby Suggs, was dead, and the sons, Howard and Buglar, had run away by the time they were thirteen years old—as soon as merely looking in a mirror shattered it (that was the signal for Buglar); as soon as two tiny hand prints appeared in the cake (that was it for Howard). (24)

In 1955, when I was ten, my father's reading went to his head.

My father's reading during that time, and for many years before and after, consisted for the most part of Life on the Mississippi. *He was a young executive in the old family firm, American Standard; sometimes he traveled alone on business. Traveling, he checked into a hotel, found a bookstore, and chose for the night's reading, after what I fancy to have been long deliberation, yet another copy of* Life on the Mississippi. *He brought all these books home. There were dozens of copies of* Life on the Mississippi *on the living-room shelves. From time to time, I read one. (25)*

Everyone had always said that John would be a preacher when he grew up, just like his father. It had been said so often that John, without ever thinking about it, had come to believe it himself. Not until the morning of his fourteenth birthday did he really begin to think about it, and by then it was too late. (26)

Chapter 7

Maintaining Interest

IN COMMON USAGE, THE WORD *ARGUMENT* CONJURES UP VISIONS OF domestic disagreements, of people engaged in heated exchanges, of lawyers attacking or defending someone in the courtroom. Indeed, the usual synonyms for *argument* are *controversy* and *dispute*. But in writing, *argument* implies the *total* art of persuasion, of convincing your readers that what you have to say is true, and keeping their interest by creating a reality so dynamic that it temporarily suspends all other realities. This lies at the heart of effective, as opposed to pedestrian, prose—nonfiction or fiction, letters or reports—and is what gives the written word its magnetic power, charisma, magic: unfolding information in a way that makes the reader want to believe, want to read on, want to know more. You do so through the intuitive but reasoned process of first establishing your thesis, and then supporting it with arrestingly detailed examples that build on each other to reach a believable outcome.

Intuition and Reason

The words *intuitive* and *reasoned* may, I realize, seem contradictory. *Intuition* is defined as "The immediate knowing of something without the conscious use of reasoning," whereas *reason* is said to be "thinking logically or analytically" (27). But when you are engaged in the reasoned process of writing, you are simultaneously involved in the intuitive, imaginative act of creating, in which the subconscious refers to your credo system, your nonreligious faith, or "the assurance of things hoped for, the conviction of things not seen" (28).

For instance, when you gather information on a subject and then select the thesis that you want to demonstrate or argue for, you do so logically; yet even as you are doing it, intuition may lead you to look into the unlikely, as well as emphasize—perhaps reject—this or that area of research. When you write, your effort to support your thesis is reasoned,

but the feelings that help you do so persuasively are fueled by your imagination, by gut sense, by hunches and guesses, as you fly by the seat of
your literary pants, sometimes coming up with thoughts that surprise
you. Your spirit is a vital component of your ability to reason.

To illustrate this general contention, suppose we take a hypothetical
example in which research has come up with the startling evidence that
while the incidence of breast cancer is, say, one in nine nationally, it happens to be one in seven in three metropolitan communities adjacent to the
mouth of a river. Since these statistics are significant, the best public
health brains are called in to study the situation. By a careful reasoning
process, they exclude all probable causes except the river, which contains
minor traces of pesticide. Then, followed by the news media, they begin
to search upstream for possible sources of contamination.

At this point, put yourself into the picture. Assume that you are not
an expert and have had little or no experience with medical subjects, but
you are curious, educated, and intelligent. You note that the three communities are all upper or upper-middle class and can afford the best of
medical care—with or without insurance. On a hunch, you look into methods used for gathering data on breast cancer and discover that the higher
figures precisely match the higher level of care; that is, more people were
getting better attention, and better attention resulted in more complete
data, which turned up more cases of breast cancer.

If you now decide to write about this, intuition again inspires your
choice of thesis: How is the evidence best presented?—to stir up controversy? challenge the use of unquestioned statistics? advocate for improved national health care programs? castigate researchers and the sen-
sation-seeking arm of the news media? Your decision. So think, but give
your spirit room to maneuver.

Daring to Be Different

Above all, dare to do something different. Respect the opinions of others,
but be fearless in your quest to come as close as possible to the truth, regardless of prevailing consensus. All it takes is one exception to invalidate a theory, no matter how important or widely accepted it is.

Take the case of a remote, impoverished backwoods community in
which all of the people were moderately retarded and considered genet-
ically impaired by inbreeding. Costly medical programs were about to be
activated to remediate the situation, when a young social worker happened to notice that everyone in the community ate mostly peeled local
tubers, cooked in various ways and occasionally fortified with a stewed

rat. Acting without authority, since her department adhered to the genetic theory, she put one of the boys with the lowest IQ on a healthful diet and found that after a few weeks he tested out at an IQ of 105, or slightly above normal. Before the experts would believe her, however, she was obliged to repeat the process with several other children, all selected at random. Her thesis that nutrition, not genetics, was involved proved to be right, and eventually she was able to help all the children, although the adults —too long impaired—remained retarded.

Care creates the strong thesis or contention, and it is inspired, intuitive.

The forms that you use to demonstrate your thesis may be diverse, but each is a function of either inductive or deductive reasoning, and none can violate the law of cause and effect without invalidating your entire argument. Claim that kissing causes baldness, and who's going to believe you? The addition of creativity to this process involves exploring probabilities and questioning widely accepted facts, struggling with the angel as Jacob did on the celestial ladder, receiving the boon while being wounded by inspiration. For instance, assume that you plan to write about what happens to people in the face of challenge, and you have narrowed your thesis to defining *challenge* as the clash between a personal goal and strong opposition to it. Since this is easy to demonstrate, the reader may simply agree and go on to something else. However, if you introduce a vulnerable thesis, such as a variation of Henri Bergson's contention that people *evolve* through challenge, you have prepared the way to suggest that problems may be opportunities in disguise, that new directions are inherent in difficulties, great accomplishments prefaced by uncertainties—that, as Arthur Willis Colton put it, "We owe almost all our knowledge not to those who have agreed, but to those who have differed" (29).

At this point—granted that problems large and small occur daily—you are curious to see how this can apply to you. Your challenge as a writer now becomes a matter of upholding your end of the bargain by presenting interesting examples in imaginative, persuasive sequence. You might tell stories about people who discovered opportunities amid frustrations, like those who developed Post-It memo pads from a glue that wouldn't work; and you could show that those who *don't* accept the challenge of problems may be consumed by them and leave the opportunity for someone else to discover.

As another case in point, let's suppose that you have decided to write about grief because you have experienced insights into it. Research leads you to advance the thesis that grief is a healing process which needs to be expressed, not repressed. Most readers might nod over this and wonder, "So what?" But if you introduce a vulnerable thesis, wide open to challenge, that repressed grief can lead to counterproductive emotional and intellectual changes (concurrently letting intuition further guide you into using linguistics as a diagnostic tool), you have invited the reader to explore a significant concept. Thereafter, you can go on to discuss the examples of, say, well-known male writers (men—far more than women—have difficulty admitting feelings of vulnerability), from Mark Twain to Ernest Hemingway, who did not recover from some great loss and were eventually undone by it because they thought that smothering grief was the manly way of handling it. Your contention might then be enhanced by comparing your examples with the work of men and women writers who talked about what happened to them and who, in time, recovered, such as Isabella Bird and C. S. Lewis.

Being Specific

In the foregoing examples, the more specific and detailed you are, the clearer and more persuasive will be your argument. This sounds self-evident, but most arguments falter or fail when the writer proceeds from one generality to another, drawing assumptions along the way, eventually reaching a pathetic conclusion that sags like a leaky air mattress. Being specific accomplishes two great things:

1. Interesting details breathe life into your writing.
2. The particulars allow you to check the accuracy of what you are trying to say.

For instance, let's suppose that you want to write about Truth versus Honesty and have decided that a fundamental difference exists between the two. If you then point out that Honesty means being trustworthy and sincere, and that Truth means conforming to reality, you have to rely on clever wording to keep your audience from falling asleep, while you have no firm specifics against which to check your message. But if you cite the *Playboy* interview—widely covered by the news at the time—in which President Jimmy Carter stated that he had, in his heart, "lusted after women," you have an opportunity to explore various possible reasons why he said it. You also have an opportunity to particularize by examining Truth and Honesty against concepts of candor, intention, naivete, intelligence, wisdom, and a host of circumstantial details. This can be compared with Rosalyn Carter's disclaimer that, "I'm sure Jimmy didn't mean that he committed adultery!" Well then, what did he mean? And what do *you* mean?

Being specific will help you clarify what you are trying to say and why you are trying to say it. Specificity brings you closer to a winning position. Above all, it will help you avoid conjuring up nice-sounding sentiments that are patently fraudulent, as in those pop songs claiming that love and marriage are concomitant. A good, solid example would at once shatter the generality, for it takes no great exercise of intelligence to discern that many stable but loveless marriages exist, as do many loving but unmarried couples.

Finding Examples

If strong supporting examples are so important, how do you find, select, and use them? One sure way is to be alert to ideas, thoughts, and incidents that intrigue you in whatever you read, hear, see, or experience. These need to be recorded (along with source or circumstance) in your notes, *as they occur,* for possible use later on. The more detailed they are, the better, and those you eventually select should be those that most clearly illustrate, in an interesting way, the point that you are trying to make. As a rule of thumb, if four examples—nonredundant—have equal merit, and you can use only three, pick the three that most strongly appeal to you, realizing that your spirit, your enthusiasm, your sense of fascination breathe excitement into your writing. The order in which you use them involves understanding *process*—the sequence in which something is done to achieve a desired effect. Thus, on looking over the examples you've chosen, you may see that one will be best as your lead, another to follow, the third to conclude.

The process exercises at the end of this chapter will help you better understand how to shape your personal approach to sequencing. They will also help you understand narrative techniques, which are as important to nonfiction as they are to fiction. While often considered a function of stories only, *narrative* in its pure sense, like process, means the order in which events are related to achieve a desired effect. This "prose painting" is based on a natural sequence of thoughts, ideas, or impressions as you try to re-create reality and come as close as possible to the way things are. The technique depends in part on how information is juxtaposed in convincing detail, without in any way falsifying cause and effect. It also depends in part on what is left out. Some published writers try to include everything, along with the proverbial kitchen sink; they fill pages to say nothing at great length, tediously, if profitably. But even with the best of intentions, no one can include "everything" (though "naturalists" like Dreiser and Dos Passos tried, with great power), and the effectiveness of what you have to say is always enhanced by what you knowingly omit. Make your writing more powerful by leaving out whatever weakens it. In short, the point you want to make is clearer when you don't present the reader with a smorgasbord of verbiage. As Hemingway put it, 90 percent of writing occurs *off* the page, and all artists are helped in this process by having a "built-in shock-proof shit-detector" (30).

A Final Thought

One final thought on maintaining interest: try putting yourself in areas—intellectual, spiritual, or emotional—where you don't belong, where you are not supposed to go, where "angels fear to tread." Taking risks may stimulate your adrenal glands, but, more important, it will excite your reader as you lead him or her into the "unsafe," even the taboo. For instance, if you have been taught that "extremism in the defense of liberty is no vice," and your reader has, too, it could be provocative to explore evidence that extremism is the enemy of liberty. Or if you have heard that "might makes right," you could be skating on thin ice by contending that the number one bomb is not the nuclear bomb but the population time bomb. Or again: what of the assertion that our religious and educational institutions lack meaning unless they, like the writer, have a clear grasp of applied ethics, the fabric of society? The whole art of persuasion involves the emotional quotient in both you and your reader.

Be bold. You're the writer. The choices are yours.

Exercises in Developing Interest

A. Process
    1. Describe your favorite fantasy; then list all aspects of it in sequenced order.
    2.   **a.** Write a self-ad for a dating magazine, identifying the sort of person you are attracted to and the sort of person who would be attracted to you.
        b. Now describe the best-case scenario and the worst-case scenario. What would you do and how would you feel if the worst one happened?
    3. You suddenly discover that you need to change your career, or intended career.
        a. List the steps that you would take to select the new career.
        b. Then list the steps that you would have to take to find it.

    c.   Go through the same process for having to find a new place in which to live.

4.   Now repeat Exercise D in Chapter 4.

B. Narrative

1.   In clear, detailed, effective sequence, write the best narrative joke that you know—one that has a beginning, middle, and end, and sets the listener up for a surprise.

2.   You have won $20 million in the lottery. Narrate the events of your first twenty-four hours as a millionaire—what would happen? What would you think, feel, say, and do?

3.   The lover of your dreams has just entered the room at an important, crowded party where you and your date are guests. Write the narrative of what happens next. What are the significant moments of cause and effect?

4.   You come home to find your lover in bed with your best friend. What would you do? Why? Create two narrative scenarios, one grim, the other hilarious. Which one do you like more? Why?

Passages for Study

In the following two examples, note that while *process* is based on the sequence in which something is done, so is *narrative*. Both depend on careful adherence to cause and effect: if *this* happens, then *that* will happen; if *this* is happening, *that* must have happened. But in *process*, which is structured like a recipe for making bread, or instructions for programming your VCR or assembling your new bike, you need to include each and every step in the sequence or order; while *narrative* conveys a sequence of events that is made believable by what is left out.

Process

(How to present your résumé)

> When the meeting opens, the contact should be reminded as to why the job seeker is there and the contact should also be thanked. "I have a high opinion of you" or "Joe Jones has told me much about your company and I think you could offer valuable advice."
>   The job seeker should also make it clear, once again, that he is not in the contact's office looking for a job. Still, the job seeker may find the contact cautious. He may even be asked, "What position are you looking for?"

If that happens, the job seeker has the perfect opportunity to present the contact with a résumé. He might say something like, "Well, one in which I can utilize my strengths. I do not really want to take up your time describing my background and experience, so I brought a copy of my résumé. I think it will give you some insight into my abilities."

Robert McDonald suggests a line such as, "Well, Mr. Jones, I would be delighted to tell you about my background but the simplest way may be for you to take a look at my résumé." The job seeker then pulls out the résumé (which is folded in his coat pocket), opens it, and slips it across the desk. "I will just sit here for a moment while you are looking at it, and if there are any questions, I would be happy to answer them."

The job seeker should remain quiet and give the contact a chance to read through the résumé. "Do not," cautions McDonald, "say another word. Let him open up. Too much talking can get you into trouble. Let the résumé trigger the questions and his response." (31)

Narrative

Marny and I were at the back door when Checkers, standing on the deck with Parker, fell in seizure through the plate glass window. He fell like a cut tree, his head shattering the glass at floor level. The impact occurred at the base of his skull. If it had been on his neck, the blow would have decapitated him. For the glass laid him open like a sword stroke.

It happened in a flash. I heard him hit, whirled to see the blood fountain as Parker cried, "Oh, my God, quick, Dad!" and in a rush I crossed the kitchen to the deck. I raised him from the glass, sat him forward to depress his breathing, drew his head back hard, and then, one by one as the blood drenched me, found in the gaping wound each severed vein and pinned it with my hands. If I had been so much as a few seconds further away, all would have been over, for the blood surged out of him so hard that it took all my strength to stem the flow. But as I knelt and got my hands onto vital points, the spray stopped.

Checkers, coming to and finding himself crushed forward in pain, his head fiercely drawn back by the hair, wailed, "What are you doing to me?"

"Don't move," I said, worried that he might panic. "Just hold as still as you can."

"But I can't see," he cried. "Am I dying? Please don't let me die."

"Breathe slow and don't cry," I told him. And he relaxed, and trusted, and I told Marny to call for help, then bring all the ice she could.

Behind me, I could hear her dial, then, unable to find the words, call wildly into the phone, "Help!" Presently the operator elicited name and address from her, and Marny and Shelley got the ice, which I had Parker stuff in a towel around Checkers' heart.

I could not possibly have held things together had it not been for Parker. The sight of so much blood unnerved him, but as he knelt there with me, he followed my directions, and after we had Checkers packed with ice, he covered the veins I could not reach. Then, as my grip weakened over the half hour it took for the ambulance to reach us, Parker's big strong hands moved in to back mine. It was an awesome thing, holding as hard as I could, seeing the blood squirt up as my muscles fatigued, feeling the back-up strength of Parker's hands against mine, feeling them weaken, too, as we both strained to hold Checkers together and talk his spirits up.

We were locked there, unmoving, in a fierce combat for Checkers' life, kneeling in the night, sweating and breathing hard as we strained against weakening muscles and the slipperiness. And then in the distance through the valley we heard the wail of the siren. The wail grew closer, and finally the ambulance, backed by a squad car, screamed down the drive. The medic, following Shelley's directions, charged through the carport around to the deck.

"Thank God," was all I could say when I saw him. (32)

Chapter 8

Ways of Concluding

The importance of leaving your reader empowered,

interested, or proactive

WE HAVE ALL SEEN OR HEARD ABOUT G*R*A*N*D O*P*E*N*I*N*G*S, SOME of them little more than plain old ordinary openings, despite the fanfare of balloons, banners, luminous paint, searchlights, and prolonged billings. But what about grand closings? Isn't the way things end worthy of as much attention as the way things begin? Unfortunately, while symphonies, funerals, and bankruptcy sales may have impressive or memorable conclusions, and some defeated presidential candidates have conceded with unexpected and therefore unforgettable grace, in writing, as in life, the inspired ending is rare. Apart from an occasional book, story, or movie, the evidence suggests that after we have said what we have to say, most of us want to get it over with as efficiently as possible, perhaps relying on some familiar method, such as the summary, recommendation, prediction, quotation, or anecdote. All of these are acceptable but tend to be overused, conventional, tedious, or cute. Some ill-conceived endings can even be turn-offs, as happens when otherwise informative, well-written commercials abruptly conclude with "Hurry!" or "Don't miss it!"—words that dispose many of us to ignore what we are supposed to feel pressured to hurry up about or not miss. Yet overemphasizing the ending isn't a good idea, either, since it may divert attention from your key point, or introduce new, unsubstantiated information. In other words—to close this paragraph—what the reader goes away with, what secures that reader's lasting impression, has much to do with the effective simplicity of your final thoughts, as well as their significance or their movingly generous spirit.

Conclusions: Three Basic Considerations

You should look to three basic considerations: (1) focusing on something interesting to think about, (2) presenting something meaningful to feel, and (3) offering something constructive to do. Leaving your reader with

at least one of these will underscore the value of what you have just said
. . . and perhaps arouse curiosity about what you will have to say in your
next work.

To exemplify, let us first consider a sample thesis. Suppose that you
have written about the way in which clothing makes a statement, projecting a sense of self and therefore affecting the reaction of others to us
and our reaction to others. Also suppose that your fundamental message
is that these reactions are based on our perception of differences, with
some differences being acceptable, others provocative or even threaten-
ing—that clothes are a form of communication that arises from appear-
ances but reflects attitudes and group affiliation. Let us further suppose
that you have selected several categories of clothing to illustrate your re-
marks and are now ready to conclude. Overused phrases like "In conclusion . . ." and "As we have seen . . ." are lame. Summarizing what you
have just said, going over and highlighting each category, is an exercise
in absurdity unless required for some academic or professional reason. If
you have said it well the first time, you hardly need to repeat yourself for
emphasis in abbreviated form. Making a recommendation or prediction
can be equally absurd, since neither has any meaningful relationship to
the subject. After all, what will you say? Urge people not to pay attention
to clothes? Prophesy the extinction of society if they do? Quotations and
anecdotes may be redundant, since you will have needed as many of
these as possible to illustrate each category—to show what people have
said and done in reaction to attire, personal or professional, throughout
the ages.

Giving your reader something interesting to think about, on the other
hand, might involve making an amusing comparison between, say, skirts
and slacks, and wondering why women have no trouble wearing slacks,
whereas men experience awkwardness about wearing skirts—unless the
circumstances are laughable, as in the movie *Mrs. Doubtfire*. On a heav-
ier note, you might pose another kind of question: Why does biker garb
make some people feel uneasy, while surfer garb does not? Given the obvious availability of a wide variety of clothing styles for both of these
sporting activities, what prompts each group to wear what it does? Why
do bikers seek to look tough, while surfers look as if they were on per-
petual vacation? Since you have already scored your key points in the
body of your thesis, provoking an interesting thought in your conclusion
offers the reader something to ponder and something to talk about with
others later on. Why, after all, *do* we react to clothes . . . or the lack of
them?

As for giving your reader something to feel, this might involve the
graphic image of people being killed for nothing more than wearing the
"wrong" gang colors, or people starving because their ethnic attire mis-
clued the drivers of relief trucks, or people being rejected by religious,

political, and educational institutions because of "unacceptable" clothing. But because your effort has been, say, to encourage people to appreciate instead of reject each other—regardless of externals—a more
forceful feeling with which to conclude would be positive, the feeling
of care: perhaps showing a sinister-looking heavy-metaler stopping to
help a bewildered old man get on a bus from which conventionally
dressed commuters had been pushing him aside. If beauty is more than
skin deep, you might conclude, then isn't the spirit of love deeper than
raiment?

Finally, giving your reader something to do is far stronger than making a "recommendation." Recommending that people stop paying so
much attention to externals has nowhere near the concluding strength of
suggesting a course of action: what each of us can do *personally* to correct
and redirect social misperceptions—misperceptions that predate the para-
ble of the Good Samaritan.

For instance, in your research, you might have learned that pressure
to conform to the patterns of one group or another begins early in
school and intensifies as puberty approaches. During this period, each
person also experiences a struggle for identity. A handy aid in both
cases is costuming: fitting in by wearing what your group does, emu-
lating your role model by dressing to look like him or her. As the emphasis on externals becomes a way of life, so does the inability to see
beyond them. Such a thought could lead you to encourage your readers
to engage in daily acts of acceptance, regardless of what some person is
or isn't wearing.

Other Ways of Concluding

To illustrate other ways of concluding, let us consider a second thesis.
Suppose you have written about the increasing number of couples who
have decided to live together without any intent to marry because they
have seen their parents painfully terminate one or more marriages. Also
assume that your basic message is that love and commitment—not legal-
ities—are what keep people together; that far too often "falling in love" is
based only on romance or lust that wears off after the daters discover
what terrible roommates they make; and that respect and friendship involve a whole lot more than a few hours of screaming sex or subnavel en-
counters. Let us further assume that you have supported your contention
by interviewing several couples and ex-couples and are now ready to
conclude. If your examples are complete, you already will have used
many quotations and anecdotes in them; summarizing what you have
just said would be pointlessly repetitious, while recommendation and
prediction bear the inherent risk of sermonizing, turning people off when

your real objective is not to scold or gloat but to open people's hearts and minds.

Instead, you might want to give your reader something to think about by wondering why certain rigid individuals and institutions have difficulty accepting that the pursuit of happiness is a personal, not social, matter. You might also wonder why unmarried cohabitation has been referred to as "living in sin," while a formal marriage is considered "sanctified," even though it may be mutually abusive, making those involved feel increasingly worthless. Or if you choose to conclude by giving your reader something to feel, you might note that the divorce rate is an abstraction whose reality is broken hearts and bewildered children, that when any relationship ends, the loss, the death of love, gives rise to unmitigated grief. Finally, giving your readers something to do could involve suggesting that they engage in open dialogue with others whose relationship preferences may seem different, unacceptable, wrong. Walk a mile, as the saying goes, in the other person's moccasins before presumptively casting judgment. It is not just loving but healthy to try to understand the seemingly strange.

Whatever you choose to do, always remember that what gives us a sense of happiness is not so much a matter of outcome as of process. The same applies to success, which also may involve accomplishment but in reality derives from loving what you do and doing what you love. Yes, it "feels good" to win a prize or a contest, but *winning*, like happiness, is an inside, ongoing job. And the importance of any ending resides in embracing thoughts, feelings, or actions that put work in clear, interesting perspective.

For the writer, a best seller is a trophy, but the real "win" is the joy of having made a welcome difference in the lives of others . . . and your own. That is what reaching a memorable ending does.

Exercises in Effective Conclusions

A. List the highlights of your life and arrange them in order of importance.
   1. Write a paragraph explaining why #1 is Number One.
   2. Think of why you sequenced the others in the order you did.
   3. Reach a conclusion about what prompts us to value one achievement over another; focus on an interesting thought, feeling, or course of action.

B. 1. Describe what you think is the *worst* thing that could happen to you socially or emotionally. List everything you would do if it happened.

2. Describe what you think is the *best* thing that could happen to you socially or emotionally. List everything you would do if it happened.

3. Now consider the good that could happen in the "worst" scenario and the worst that could happen in the "best," and draw a conclusion about what makes things seem good or bad; use an interesting thought, feeling, or course of action.

C. 1. What is the best movie you've ever seen? Rewrite and improve the conclusion.

2. Now do the same for what you consider to be a top short story and a first-rate article from a magazine or newspaper.

D. Here is a hypothetical situation: You are on a commercial jetliner that has been skyjacked. The pilot and co-pilot die trying to overcome the skyjacker, who then at random picks you to pilot the plane while he points a gun at the passengers. Although you have never flown an airplane before, you manage to hold this one steady and make voice contact with controllers at the skyjacker's designated airport. They talk you down, and you then disable the skyjacker as everyone cheers.

Write the conclusion
1. As a short story
2. As a magazine article
3. As an essay for an English class

Passages for Study

Endings need to be satisfying or surprising yet derived from what has gone before or has been developed from the start. The following two conclusions happen to be the effective endings of superb work by major authors. Your challenge is to try to surmise what has already been written that makes each one work. In other words, create the situation that leads up to the conclusion.

> *Then when that was over, Jason and Sara sat in darkness where their bed had been, and it was colder than ever. The fire the kitchen table had made seemed wonderful to them—as if what they had never said, and what could not be, had its life, too, after all.*
>
> *But Sara trembled, again pressing her hard knees against her breast. In the return of winter, or the night's cold, something strange, like fright, or dependency, a sensation of complete helplessness, took possession of her. All at once, without turning her head, she spoke.*

"Jason . . ."
A silence. But only for a moment.
"Listen," said her husband's uncertain voice.
They held very still, as before, with bent heads.
Outside, as though it would exact something further from their
lives, the whistle continued to blow. (33)

I was leaving the South to fling myself into the unknown, to meet
other situations that would perhaps elicit from me other responses.
And if I could meet enough of a different life, then, perhaps, gradu-
ally and slowly I might learn who I was, what I might be. I was
not leaving the South to forget the South, but so that some day I
might understand it, might come to know what its rigors had done
to me, to its children. I fled so that the numbness of my defensive
living might thaw out and let me feel the pain—years later and far
away—of what living in the South had meant.

Yet deep down, I knew that I could never really leave the
South, for my feelings had already been formed by the South, for
there had been slowly instilled into my personality and conscious-
ness, black though I was, the culture of the South. So, in leaving, I
was taking a part of the South to transplant in alien soil, to see if
it could grow differently, if it could drink of new and cool rains,
bend in strange winds, respond to the warmth of other suns, and,
perhaps, to bloom. . . . And if that miracle ever happened, then I
would know that there was yet hope in that southern swamp of de-
spair and violence, that light could emerge even out of the blackest
of the southern night. I would know that the South too could over-
come its fear, its hate, its cowardice, its heritage of guilt and
blood, its burden of anxiety and compulsive cruelty.

With ever watchful eyes, and bearing scars, visible and invisi-
ble, I headed North, full of a hazy notion that life could be lived
with dignity, that the personalities of others should not be vio-
lated, that men should be able to confront other men without fear
or shame, and that if men were lucky in their living on earth they
might win some redeeming meaning for their having struggled and
suffered here beneath the stars. (34)

Chapter 9

Revision

Constructive approaches to reviewing

and rewriting your work

MANY OF US HAVE BEEN TAUGHT TO THINK THAT IF WHAT WE'VE WRITTEN needs to be revised, something must be wrong with it. Not so. Creativity may begin with the first draft, but the creative process goes on until the text stops changing, usually after numerous revisions. To submit your work before you reach that point can be embarrassing.

For example, writing in the August 5, 1992, *Los Angeles Times*, Richard Ben Cramer was quoted as saying:

> <u>*Anybody who's*</u> *worth a damn* <u>*has*</u> *done something in* <u>*their*</u> *life that* <u>*they*</u> *can't explain to 2,000 reporters in 20 seconds. (underlining added)*

Since it is an interesting observation, the editors wisely used it as a heading; apparently they were unaware that Cramer had switched from singular to plural twice in his twenty-one-word sentence. (See note 13, p. 90.) Given time to revise, he might more effectively have said in fourteen words:

> *Anyone worth a damn has done something that can't be easily explained to reporters.*

Sloppy Communication—and How to Avoid It

Unfortunately, the great rush to get things done today has made verbal slop far from random, and the more that people are subjected to sloppy communication, the greater the tendency to consider slop acceptable, to think that it's sensible to say, as happened on the *Geraldo* television show of August 30, 1993, "The baby never did nothing to nobody," or to write, "I know my brother better than you" (Better than I know you? Better than you know him?), or "He kept a secret from his family that almost killed him" (Which almost killed him, family or secret?), or "A structure under construction is destroyed when a plumbers [sic] torch ignites the flames" (35). (Don't torches usually ignite *structures*?) There also have been instances where, in haste, a writer has devoted an entire article to *Chile*, the country, when what was meant was *chili*, the food, or used *gantlet* instead of *gauntlet* without pausing to check spelling and definition in the dictionary.

The shame is not so much what happens to the English language in such cases, for English, always vibrantly alive and changing, will survive; the shame is what happens to people's minds when they become accustomed to unreason stemming from lack of care. Taking time to revise can eliminate a lot of confusion and improve the ideas themselves, as well as strengthen the ways in which they are expressed.

More important, revision can increase your power of thought; for every time that you attempt to "re-see" what you have written, you are *rethinking* it, too. Also, every attempt to clarify what you have said deepens your understanding of what you are trying to say. Indeed, the quality of the result derives from the quality of the means, and the quality of the means arises from the reflective labor of honing your words. In contrast, the increasing superficiality of much that emanates from our twentieth-century Tower of Babel stands as cacophonous evidence that "fastfood" communication produces more verbiage than we can readily digest or avoid. This leads to difficulty in listening to, hearing, or understanding each other.

Revision eliminates the tendency to dysfunctional overtalk, and several strategies can enhance your creative process of revision. The first and probably the most effective is to run off a clean copy of your manuscript. With a computer, this is effortless. If you prefer to handwrite, then you should type your copy; or, if you prefer to typewrite, then *re*type your copy. Next, using a pencil, mark up the draft as heavily as possible, changing and rearranging words, sentences, and paragraphs as you go over your manuscript. Do this at least three times. Finally, after setting your work aside overnight, rewrite it, make another clean copy, and repeat the mark-up process, "keeping on keeping on" until not even a comma can be usefully changed. At this point, comparing your initial discovery draft with your final or submission draft, you will have a direct measure of the importance of revision, not only to your reader but to yourself.

Reading Aloud and Peer Comment

Two other strategies go right along with the first: reading aloud and peer comment. Reading aloud what you have written gives you a chance to hear your words, not just see them. Often, phrases that look right don't sound right. Hearing your work (it can also be helpful to have someone else read it to you), even responding to it aloud, can sharpen your editorial ear *and* eye, as well as your listening skills.

Peer comment, on the other hand, requires that you find someone who will be perceptively honest with you—blunt if necessary, but never mean. Forget about the possibility of having your feelings hurt. A good critic, like a good editor, is a mirror to your work. If you don't like what you see, change what you have written—don't berate the mirror or yourself. Sensitivities and ego are not at issue here; the quality of your work is. The challenge is to do your best, where you are, with what you have. Someone who offers you only praise and pleasantries is of little use, as is someone who incessantly carps on your presumed faults and is incapable of identifying any of your real strengths.

Changing Your Thesis—or Your Point of View

Additionally, whenever the pressures of time are great, you should consider two other forms of revision that can be done by reoutlining: (1) revising your outline by changing your thesis and (2) revising your outline by changing your point of view. For instance, let's consider the second topic discussed in Chapter 8. Suppose that you have decided to write about the pros and cons of unmarried cohabitation. Let us further suppose that you have researched the subject, have chosen the thesis that living together is wrong, and have prepared to illustrate your contention with examples of unmarried relationships that failed. Suddenly you realize that the fail-rate of unmarried relationships is actually lower than the fail-rate of married relationships—that something else must be involved. At this point you change your thesis to indicate that relationships without commitment are fatally flawed; a subsequent rethink suggests that what you really mean is that any relationship without love is at risk. You are now in position to revise your outline to support your new contention before you have even started your first draft, which must, for various reasons, also be your last.

Much the same applies to the process of revising your outline by changing your point of view. How many points of view are there on this subject? To name a few (and omitting politicians): your church, school, peers, and parents may all have differing, often harshly judgmental opinions about living together. If you have taken the position that cohabitation is wrong, have done so from a religious or moral standpoint, and then have realized that the point of view has limitations that require you to shift to the way peer victims of divorce may see things, you have created the conditions that call for revising your outline to support your contention that too many relationships tend to be formed *and* dissolved on the basis of sexual gratification, or lack thereof.

Regardless of how you revise, always be sure to cross-check your argument with each revision, for the key to ensuring your credibility is alertness to the law of the universe: cause and effect. Anyone who claims that a given effect was created by a cause with no plausible connection to the effect, or who claims that a stated cause will result in an unrelated effect, can get away with it only as long as the basic assumption goes unchallenged—a concept that many politicians fail to grasp. To wit: those who claim to have the absolute answer for democracy are in fact the greatest enemies of democracy, for absolute rightness and democracy are opposites. Indeed, absolutes tend to be destructive in any field, from religion to science. Writers, above all, must be proponents of open, unbiased expression, recognizing that backing up what you have to say is not a matter of force or exclusion but of reason. The strength of your reasoning can be greatly enhanced by multiple revisions, as well as by keeping notes in which you record and debate your ideas, your views, your opinions.

Strong Writing—Writing to Express, Not Impress

While you are revising, always remember that the power of words is based on their effectiveness, not their length or complexity. Language is meant to transfer thought as clearly and meaningfully as possible from your mind to the reader's mind. Yet often writers are tempted to display their vocabularies, to impress rather than express. Thus we may hear someone pompously telling us to "cleave to the Rhadamanthine" instead of saying "be just," or talking about an "eclectic vaticinator" instead of a "selective prophet." The classic joke about polysyllabic meaninglessness is the rendition of "Twinkle, twinkle little star, how I wonder what you are" that goes: "Scintillate, scintillate, diminutive astral body, how I interrogate the nature of your celestial existence." When this happens in

jingles, we can laugh; when it happens to communications in our institutions, we may want to vomit. But when we find it happening in our
own work, we need to revise, to find out what we are trying to obscure
and why, for, according to Yale studies (36), the twelve most persuasive
words in the English language are all simple:

you	money	save
now	easy	free
guarantee	love	discovery
results	health	proven

The list does not include such real persuaders as *sin, sale, sex,* and *fun,* but
you can see that words that reach the reader are rarely complex, although
they may be used to express complex ideas.

Effective and affective sentences are based on such words. To revise
that: *strong sentences are clear.* One of the best ways to develop them is to
take a well-known line from a recognized writer's work and try to revise
and improve it. For instance, consider William Faulkner's statement from
his Nobel Prize acceptance speech, "The basest of all things is to be
afraid." What does it mean? How can you write a better line without
using someone else's words, like Franklin Roosevelt's, "We have nothing
to fear but fear itself"?

Now try it with a few other quotations (37) until you feel yourself
gaining in confidence:

Emily Dickinson—*Publication is the auction of the Mind of Man.*

Thomas Carlyle—*A well-written life is almost as rare as a well-
spent one.*

Oscar Wilde—*The difference between journalism and literature is
that journalism is unreadable and literature is not read.*

Robert Frost—*You can be a little ungrammatical if you come from the
right part of the country.*

Katherine Anne Porter—*It is as hard to find a neutral critic as it is
a neutral country in time of war.*

H. G. Wells—*No passion in the world is equal to the passion to alter
someone else's draft.*

Willa Cather—*Most of the basic material a writer works with is ac-
quired before the age of fifteen.*

Punctuation and Grammar

Rethinking sentences, groping for stronger words, the power words, can be an important and enjoyable excercise for you, but checking punctuation and grammar is also part of revision. At one time or another, most of us have felt bewildered or intimidated by the "rules and regulations"; we have assumed that if we sprinkled a few commas and other punctuation marks here and there on the page, it would look better, somehow more "official." But if grammar is the history of usage, rather than the dictator of it, so is punctuation. Both are supposed to help clarify what we say, not confuse people. For example, try to read the following line:

that that is is that that is not is not is not that it it is

Without punctuation, who knows what it means? But if we add punctuation, let's see what happens:

That that is, is. That that is not, is not. Is not that it? It is.

Punctuation marks in unhelpful places can also cause confusion:

Every lady in the land
Has twenty nails on each hand.
Five and twenty on hands and feet;
This is true without deceit.

The writer is either lying or making a preposterous joke. But let's see what happens when we change the punctuation:

Every lady in the land
Has twenty nails; on each hand
Five, and twenty on hands and feet.
This is true without deceit.

The quatrain may not be any better, but now at least it makes sense—a sense not evident until we introduced visual (and thus "audible") pauses.
    Punctuation can be useful in more subtle ways, too. For instance, consider the following sentence in which commas have been shifted to modify the emphasis:

"O.K.," I agreed and, with a smile, slept.

"O.K.," I agreed, and with a smile slept.

The first separates *smile* from *slept* in a way that alters the feel of the line and might be crucial if, say, the speaker happened to be recovering from grief. The tempo of the two sentences also differs, as you can hear by reading them aloud.

Paragraphs and Transitions

If sentences are like details in a painting, paragraphs may be compared to unified and integrated sections of it. Each presents a thought, view, or concept that is related to the whole. A paragraph scores because the sentences in it are lively and because it is an interesting and effective contribution to the overall thesis.

To test this, first check back to the subject in Chapter 5 and your tentative answers to the journalist's questions. Then write a paragraph fully explaining your definition of pornography to a Tibetan monk. Next see if the paragraph is improved by revising it to make your listener a cloistered nun. Try this again, first defining *pornography* to your parents, next to a judge, and finally to a gathering of librarians. The most exuberant of these attempts is the one that will stand alone—delightfully. But if it is part of a larger picture that you are painting, you need to integrate it with the whole by showing its relationship to (1) your message and (2) the next section.

The interconnections are what we call *transitions* (as exemplified in the shift from the foregoing paragraph to this one). Associations are involved. The simpler they are, the better. The best professionals make transitions so deftly that we are hardly aware that it has happened. For example, in *The Old Man and the Sea*, Hemingway takes us from one time and action to another in two swift, seemingly simple strokes: "The old man looked at the fish constantly to make sure it was true. It was an hour before the first shark hit him." The complexity of the transition is so stark, so cut to the bone, that it looks easy, although the author may have spent hours achieving it, throwing out more cumbersome attempts.

Transitions are the hallmark of excellent writing. The good ones don't show. They are inspired, not methodical. They are based on what is left out yet convey the whole. Try identifying a few in the work of writers like Jane Austen, Ann Petry, or Barbara Pym. Then see how effortlessly Peter Hoeg does it in *Smilla's Sense of Snow* (38):

> *Even in the examining room, which is painted like a living room, they've brought in a couple of floor lamps, and a green plant is trying to keep up its courage.*
> *There's a white sheet over Isaiah.*

Here the transition is not a matter of time but of focus. With effective ease, our attention has been shifted to a corpse as the writer skates the surface of deep feelings, which we sense without having to be told.

A Commitment to Communication

Genius, as Thomas Edison once remarked, is 1 percent inspiration and 99 percent perspiration. Those who seek to improve thoughts and the way we record them need to make a spiritual commitment to the process, to realize that there was a time when only the privileged few had access to the inner sanctum of communications. History tells us that, in early civilization, all communications were oral, that myths and legends were passed on by word of mouth from the chosen few to the chosen few. Then came writing, which only the priests could understand, controlling what was transferred and how it was interpreted. But the advent of printing and movable type paved the way to translations in the vernacular, which gave access to all.

To understand your commitment to the written word and to express it carefully and caringly, without in any way compromising the integrity of your quest for the Truth, is, therefore, to recognize a special honor that is yours, as we now enter the new age of the information superhighway.

Parting Shots: An Exercise in Revision

1. Research the topic of "challenge"—its meaning and feeling. Look up examples of your definition and take notes as you go along.
2. Decide on your thesis and prepare an outline on how you plan to illustrate it.
3. Show separate copies of your outline to three acquaintances whose opinions you trust, and ask for their comments.
4. Broaden the scope of your research on "challenge" to include other perspectives, such as the news, literature, television, movies, sports, and business.
5. Revise your thesis and outline, seeking further comment as you do so.
6. Write your discovery draft as quickly as possible by fleshing out your outline, not stopping until you have reached a conclusion.
7. Retype the discovery draft in a form suitable to show to one of the three people who commented on your outline.
8. Get a second opinion from a new source.

9. Focus and deepen your research.
10. Rewrite your discovery draft and seek further comment.
11. Set this aside and do something else.
12. Revise your work until it stops changing.
13. Now you're ready to clean-type your submission draft.

Passage for Study

Here is the first paragraph from *The Hero Within* (39), a best-selling book that offers insights into individual life journeys. Since this passage is difficult to improve, your challenge is to rewrite it three times to see if you can create what two friends think is a more effective version.

> *Heroes take journeys, confront dragons, and discover the treasure of their true selves. Although they may feel very alone during the quest, at its end their reward is a sense of community with themselves, with other people, and with the earth. Every time we confront death-in-life we confront a dragon, and every time we choose life over nonlife and move deeper into the ongoing discovery of who we are, we vanquish the dragon; we bring new life to ourselves and to our culture. We change the world. The need to take the journey is innate in the species. If we do not risk, if we play prescribed social roles instead of taking our journeys, we feel numb; we experience a sense of alienation, a void, an emptiness inside. People who are discouraged from slaying dragons internalize the urge and slay themselves by declaring war on their fat, their selfishness, or some other attribute they think does not please. Or they become ill and have to struggle to get well. In shying away from the quest, we experience nonlife and, accordingly, we call forth less life in the culture.*

Chapter 10

Ethical Considerations

The importance of applied ethics to you, your

writing, and the well-being of others

FEW OF US WOULD DISAGREE THAT ETHICAL STANDARDS ARE ESSENTIAL not only to communications today but to the very survival of society itself—local, national, international. It is also obvious, as intimated in Chapters 2, 4, and 7, that when ethical standards are compromised, the very soul of our communications is at risk, and individual behavior becomes self-serving, as some vital spirit evaporates from our institutions—political, educational, religious. Because these hazards have become potentially cataclysmic, it is imperative that the winning writer understand the fundamentals of applied ethics in order both to survive and, one hopes, to prevail.

But what *is* ethics, apart from just another course in philosophy, or a word that we sometimes use without giving it much thought? And, granted its importance, can we agree on a universal definition, one that people everywhere could accept?

Ethics—Some Definitions

In an effort to arrive at an answer, let us first review a few existing definitions. *Webster's New World Dictionary*, for instance, states that ethics is "the study of standards of conduct and moral judgment"; but Aristotle observed that ethics was practical, Nietzsche advanced the notion that the desire for power underlies morality, Ayn Rand held that it was all a matter of self-interest, and Confucius maintained that it contributed to good human relations. More specifically, Kant believed that concepts without precepts were empty; the New Testament proposed the Golden Rule, or consideration for others; scholars may argue that ethics involves obedience to the unenforceable; Kabat-Zinn states (40) that, "You cannot have harmony without a commitment to ethical behavior"; and then we find a vice-president of the United States discussing "family values" without being entirely clear about whose family, or what values.

None of this brings us any closer to a universally acceptable or workable definition. Although we may all agree that ethics helps us distinguish right from wrong, what some people consider right may appear wrong to others. To wit: racial and/or religious intermarriage—even marriage between people whose ages differ widely—can be frowned upon in one society and approved of in another. What is upheld as wrong in one period of history may be considered right in the next, as evidenced by shifts in attitudes concerning sexuality, divorce, abortion, and the like. The code of ethics for one profession, say the FBI, would not be suitable for another profession, such as medicine.

Indeed, it may be an insurmountable challenge to come up with a definition that people everywhere can agree on, but for a moment let's say that *ethical practices honor responsibilities, respect the rights of others, uphold the spirit of truth, and proceed on a course that is not only just but fair*. Implicit in this is a modification of the Golden Rule: *do unto others as they would like to be done unto*. That is, applied ethics is very much a function of what you do and don't do, both of which are influenced by communications— by what is written, spoken, or viewed.

Deceptive Practices

To illustrate the concept, let us consider a few key areas, starting with industry and using the automotive industry as an example. We can go back to the days when auto-makers sold cars that had defects known to be hazardous, yet as industrial giants felt powerful enough to consider the loss of lives less important than the loss of money needed to correct flawed engineering.

Such a course failed our definition on all counts. It shirked responsibilities, scorned the rights of others, engaged in deception, and was both unjust and unfair. It was also stupid business, affecting not only the automotive industry but the integrity of industry in general, as well the nation's sense of self-respect, until attention to ethical practices in some areas (salaries, political action committees, and environmental considerations excepted) restored a competitive edge. The attitude that what's right is a matter of custom or of what you can get away with affects society as a whole, and this unethical climate was endorsed by writers who accepted pay to write the ads that presented the defective car as a social or sexual asset, when in reality it was a death trap.

Far from being random, such deceptive practices are widespread, as revealed in a list (41) of examples of misleading, unfair, and irresponsible advertising compiled by the Center for Science in the Public Interest, a Washington-based consumer organization. The advertisements cited had (1) misrepresented the dates for low airfares; (2) conveyed the impression that drinking a certain beer would elevate its drinker to the back seat of a limo; (3) obscured the real cost of car leases; (4) claimed that a fruit juice was made with only real fruit, when it was mostly artificial; (5) tried to sell gasoline as "environmentally friendly"; (6) promoted a "no-fee" Visa credit card that actually charged high fees; (7) portrayed cigarette smoking as "cool" or sexually attractive. And so on. And so what? one might ask—except for the fact that flooding the media with falsehood (the Ninth Commandment against bearing false witness notwithstanding) reinforces the notion that *any*thing goes as long as it makes money. If so, then where is the ethical distinction between making money selling something that will kill somebody and going right out and directly killing somebody for money?

Ethical values don't begin to erode on the family level, as commonly thought. Rather, the erosion begins at the leadership level, where the information is produced that parents and children read, hear, and view, in media controlled by money from advertising that is loaded with hidden persuaders. The media have already begun to stage stories, falsify reports, conduct polls that foster bias, and create "news" in the name of luring, controlling, and manipulating people. This is not to suggest that we need censorship—far from it. But we do need enforceable ethical standards in our communications in order to reverse the corrosive impact on families; for when family units falter, successive generations of children suffer, and the costs of healing are enormous and can take years to bring about.

Thus, we need to consider education, the hallowed halls in which we are supposed to learn how to think, how to reason, how to make sense of experience, as the written word and its meanings are transferred from one generation to the next in the learning process. Unfortunately, a persistant emphasis on rote memorization of information needed to pass tests makes peer group activities far more interesting than instruction. Few courses on any level—from math to language instruction—incorporate applied ethics. This makes it common for those entering the classroom to believe that what you don't know can't hurt you, while what you do know can. In the absence of written communication dealing with the ethical use of knowledge and information, what is learned about right and wrong becomes a matter of observing what isn't taught—grades based on favoritism and sex, behavior that helps you fit in with your peers. As William K. Kilpatrick puts it (42), instead of teaching values, schools have been turning out moral illiterates. Why? Perhaps because the greater influence is from what is being written for movies, TV, and computer games that ennoble violence and other forms of debased human behavior, equating it with "fun." In whatever caters to human depravity, the winning writer refuses to participate, instead proffering the example of ethical alternatives. For writing should be an ethical transaction, a caring effort to discover and share values that change the way we see things.

Promoting Ethical Values

Could government be of any help? Probably not, given the prevalence of witchhunts, attacks on individuals instead of issues, party bias, trumped up charges in the name of winning at any cost, and the pressures of monied interests that make partisan politics a hotbed of unethical behavior. But that does not signify. What does are things that you as winning writer can do to advance ethical concepts in our communications.

As for religion, it might be of some influence, except that religious pronouncements can be used to support less than holy ambitions. How often has history witnessed people killing and being killed in the name of God? of God's name being used in vain for personal reasons, compromised for private advantage? of churches promoting overpopulation or the degradation of women? Depending on where you open the Bible, you can find all manner of unethical activities—incest, theft, murder, blood sacrifice, symbolic cannibalism, token emasculation—whose presumed sanctity has led to abusive actions. Those who wrote the Bible and other ancient religious texts were men—male priests who could conceive of a male God rightfully doing unrighteous things, such as killing a helpless and innocent baby in order to punish David and Bathsheba (2 Samuel 12:14). While the grandeur of many religious documents, such as Psalm 139 or 1 John 4:16, derives from the tender magnificence of their ethical statements, these can be set aside in favor of antiabortion rhetoric or dogmatic prattle with which this or that group can safely agree.

Next, we come to medicine, whose practices are founded on upholding the value of life and whose ideals might offer society ethical examples—but usually don't. For instance, the American Medical Association Code of Ethics firmly advances the concept that *letting* someone die is all right, but *helping* someone die is not. Such a view can result in letting someone lie in a coma for years, or lead to exhaustive, costly, futile, and painful efforts to prolong life for no apparent humane reason. Who makes money under such circumstances? Certainly not the patient's family. Whenever any profession establishes an edict that someone else has to pay for, you as winning writer have a responsibility to examine who has what to gain, and why, especially in matters involving the touchstone of gain and loss: life and death.

Skipping over the law, which at times appears to be devoted to manipulating its own laws, we might look to athletics and hope that our "heroes" will offer us some shining example. Few do, and the industry itself appears to be single-mindedly and simple-mindedly devoted to big money, fabricated stories, and "winning as the only thing," while failing to perceive what real winning is all about: looking to what you can give, not get. Real winning is ethical; real winning honors responsibilities, respects the rights of others, upholds the truth, is voluntarily just and fair.

In the absence of real winning, we find those who have fished the seas dead, destroyed fertile land, polluted the air, sickened the environment, then turned around and expected somebody else to do something about it.

In the absence of real winning, we find people who want to gain the world by destroying it, losing their souls in the process and then blaming what happened on someone else.

Second chances are an illusion. What the winning writer does *now* is what counts. You, as you express yourself, are crucial to this process.

Avoiding False Information

Several precepts can help you identify and avoid false information, flawed points of view, misuse of selective words, staged news, and trumped up claims. Two are focal. The first involves recognizing current applications of an old formula: $F + H = P$—stir up Fear, add someone or something to Hate, and this gives Power to those who do the stirring and adding. Adolf Hitler was the most notorious user of this formula, and it also has a few flaming examples extant in feuds, internecine conflicts, gang wars, trade wars, partisan politics, and various "movements." All are characterized by an almost obscene negative energy, sugarcoated with sentiment. The first signal that precipitating information is corrupt is a sense of anxiety associated with growing antipathy for the hate object, which can be another group but is often nothing more than some presumed personal inadequacy, such as your body, mind, or social standing. The manipulator is usually someone who seems to be "the good guy," there to help you out—out of money, out of power, out of choices.

The second precept involves understanding the *percepts* of Critical Thinking that can help you evaluate the information you receive and the information you wish to convey. Daniel D. Chiras of the University of Denver (43) considers eleven principles crucial:

1. Be sure to gather complete information.
2. Define as well as understand all terms.

3. Question the methods by which facts were derived.
4. Question the conclusions drawn from facts.
5. Look for hidden assumptions and biases.
6. Question the source of facts.
7. Don't expect all of the answers.
8. Examine the big picture.
9. Examine multiple causes and effects, and be wary of simple answers.
10. Watch out for thought-stoppers or gut-level appeals not based on reason.
11. Evaluate the influence of your own bias and values.

To these we might add the need to choose your words and point of view with ethical care, for intention is as vital as procedure. But even exercising some of these principles would prompt you to challenge, say, an article that, without hard evidence, blamed childhood behavior on genetics or inborn biology, not improper parenting. As ethical care and alertness will shield you from misinformation or disinformation, it will also enhance your work, your goals, your life . . . and our world.

Good luck!

Notes

1. Albert Einstein, *Relativity: The Special and The General Theory* (New York: Crown, 1961).

2. John Burnett, ed. & trans., *Early Greek Philosophy* (London: A&C Black Ltd., 1930).

3. Denis E. Waitley, *The Psychology of Winning* (Chicago: Nightingale-Conant Corporation, 1978).

4. Joseph Campbell, *The Power of Myth* (New York: Doubleday, 1988).

5. William Strunk, Jr., & E. B. White, *The Elements of Style*, 3rd ed. (New York: Macmillan, 1979).

6. George Orwell, "Politics and the English Language," *Shooting an Elephant and Other Essays* (San Diego: Harcourt Brace Jovanovich, 1974).

7. James Charlton, ed., *Writer's Quotation Book* (New York: Pushcart Press, 1980).

8. Diane Ackerman, *A Natural History of the Senses* (New York: Random House, 1990), p. 80.

9. Annie Dillard, *Pilgrim at Tinker Creek* (New York: Harper & Row, 1974), p. 61.

10. Robin White, "The Forgotten Minority," Scripps-Howard feature, April 1985.

11. Robin White, "Backpacker Sketches," *Per/Se Magazine*, Vol. 3, No. 2, 1969, pp. 28–29.

12. Robin White, *Be Not Afraid* (New York: Dial Press, 1972), pp. 115–116.

13. Jon Kabat-Zinn, *Wherever You Go, There You Are* (New York: Hyperion, 1994), p. 5. Scholars revising the Bible to use inclusive language have also been troubled by singular/plural confusion—for example,

"Those who lose their life shall find it," which assumes that several people have only one life between them.

14. Lincoln often succeeded by using his sense of humor. In this instance, as a lawyer, he reportedly won a case by concluding his summation to the jury with the punch line from this country joke, which the jurors knew: "So as you can see, my learned opponent has *made a good observation but reached the wrong conclusion.*" He later told the joke when questioned by reporters.

15. Bret Sporich, *Pasadena Star-News,* January 27, 1994, p. B3.

16. Brian Tracy, *The Psychology of Achievement* (Chicago: Nightingale-Conant Corporation, 1987).

17. Kenneth Turan, *Los Angeles Times,* February 4, 1994, p. F1.

18. Ernest Hemingway, *The Old Man and the Sea* (New York: Scribner, 1952), p. 30.

19. Robin White, *Men & Angels* (New York: Harper, 1961), p. 1.

20. Ernest Hemingway, "The Short Happy Life of Francis Macomber," in *The Short Stories of Ernest Hemingway* (New York: Modern Library, 1938), p. 102.

21. Jean-Paul Sartre, "The Wall," in Charles Neider, ed., *Great Short Stories* (New York: Rinehart, 1950), p. 387.

22. Robin White, *All in Favor Say No* (New York: Farrar Straus, 1964), p. 3.

23. Charlton, *Writer's Quotation Book,* p. 45.

24. Toni Morrison, *Beloved* (New York: New American Library, 1987), p. 3.

25. Annie Dillard, *An American Childhood* (New York: BOMC, 1987), p. 6.

26. James Baldwin, *Go Tell It on the Mountain* (New York: Laurel, 1985), p. 11.

27. *Webster's New World Dictionary,* 1987.

28. Hebrews 11:1.

29. An unverified quote attributed to the late Arthur Willis Colton (1868–1943), author of *The Delectable Mountains* (1901), *The Belted Seas* (1905), and *Harps Hung Up in Babylon* (1907), a writer of note who remains unappreciated.

30. Charlton, *Writer's Quotation Book,* p. 36.

31. Ron Tepper, *Power Resumes* (New York: Wiley, 1989), p. 48.

32. White, *Be Not Afraid,* pp. 151–153.

33. Eudora Welty, "The Whistle," in *Curtain of Green* (New York: Harcourt Brace, 1941), p. 120.

34. Richard Wright, *Black Boy* (New York: Harper & Brothers, 1966), pp. 284–285.

35. *Los Angeles Times,* November 11, 1992, Metro Section, p. 1.

36. L. M. Boyd, *San Francisco Chronicle,* date unknown.

37. Charlton, *Writer's Quotation Book,* pp. 32, 37, 56, 61, 63.

38. Peter Hoeg, *Smilla's Sense of Snow* (New York: Farrar Straus, 1993).

39. Carol S. Pearson, *The Hero Within* (New York: Harper & Row, 1989), p. 1.

40. Kabat-Zinn, *Wherever You Go, There You Are,* p. 47.

41. *Los Angeles Times,* January 18, 1994, p. D-1.

42. William K. Kilpatrick, "Turning Out Moral Illiterates," *Los Angeles Times,* July 20, 1993, Metro Section, p. 7.

43. Daniel D. Chiras, "Teaching Critical Thinking Skills in the Biology and Environmental Science Classroom," *The American Biology Teacher,* Vol. 54, No. 8, November–December 1992, p. 464.

Nuts & Bolts—
An Appendix

Focusing on the mechanics of writing before engaging in the actual process of writing can be a bit like having to identify all the nuts and bolts in a car before learning to drive. But there are some key points that anyone aspiring to become a winning writer would do well to bear in mind.

They range from the amusing to the embarrassing and are, in my opinion, best approached in the spirit of laughter. For instance, there may be only three words that lovers hate to hear, "Honey, I'm home!" but there is a long list of hilarious errors that writers hate to find marked because they are so easily avoidable yet often occur in haste born of pressure.

Let's begin by considering the misplaced modifier, using the line, "I hit him in the eye," and inserting the word "only" at various points:

Only I hit him in the eye.

I **only** hit him in the eye.

I hit **only** him in the eye.

I hit him **only** in the eye.

I hit him in the **only** eye.

I hit him in the eye **only.**

As you can see (unless someone has hit you in an only eye), each shift of the modifier conveys a different meaning and emphasis. Being aware of this as you write and revise your work is to your advantage in making sure that what you are saying is what you mean, that what you mean is what you are saying.

But there are other basic checkpoints useful in effectively reaching your reader, not unintentionally confusing him or her. All are drawn from student papers, and I cite them in a random order that I refer to as Alphabet Soup because of the call letters I use in preparing critiques. When you are reviewing someone else's work, the list can save you a lot of time in an entertaining, nonjudgmental way, and it leaves more space to offer comment.

LF (Lard Factor)—using many words to say something that could be said better or more clearly using fewer words. Excessive verbiage sometimes looks impressive, but, like fat in hamburger, it cooks out, often making it hard to find the meat. Examples:

I decided to discontinue my employment. Why not just say "I quit"?

He had the intention of shooting. Or perhaps "He meant to shoot."

The driver had an accident with a pedestrian causing fatality. More to the point would be "The driver accidentally killed a pedestrian."

He is a quiet person, often stoic with his feelings, and many times remains to himself. In simplification: "He is shy."

Statistics show that the alarming rate about AIDS is real and the number of AIDS patients is dramatically rising. Removing the lard, we have: "The rapid spread of AIDS is alarming."

Now see what you can do with the following sentence:

She tries to tell us in her own way of a personal account that in this stereotypical world hairdo makes the woman.

RD (Redundant)—Like the lard factor, redundancies also use too many words, but unlike the LF, they unnecessarily reinforce what is being said. For instance, the word *unique* comes from the Latin *unus*, ("one") and means "one of a kind; without equal." Thus it is redundant to say *very unique, most unique,* or *absolutely unique,* although the unaware writer sometimes does so for presumed emphasis. Consider the following examples:

The store had a free gift for me. Anything that one receives as a gift is presumed to be free, yet sales campaigns rarely feature just gifts.

Clothing is worn externally on our bodies. Where else is clothing worn if not on the body? and if on the body, can it be internal?

They were united together. Is it possible to be united separately?

Return the items back. Since *return* means "send back," you can either return the items, or you can send them back.

He had no self-respect for himself. Self-respect is already for the self, making the last two words redundant.

The only main end result is death. If death is the end result, why do we need "only main"? Are there other, lesser end results?

My heart was racing at an extremely fast pace. Presumably, one's heart does not race at a slow pace, and, unless there are degrees of cardiac agitation, *extremely* is already implied.

Here is a sentence for you to work on, identifying and cutting the redundancy:

For a girl, growing up at puberty is a most significant change, more than anything else.

DP (Dangling Participle)—Far from referring to something to hang from your rearview mirror, this is an introductory participle phrase that is not logically connected to the noun that follows. Examples:

Leaping into the saddle, the horse took off.

Being a new disease, what is known about AIDS is little.

Living in this world, shame will be brought to an individual.

Walking up the street, the house came into view.

Approaching the disturbance, a crowd formed behind him.

Now try rewriting each of the sentences so that the reader will know who or what is doing the leaping, being, living, walking, and approaching.

XA (Incorrect Antecedent)— This category also includes pronoun disagreement (PD) but has been broadened to show how phrases can sometimes be sequenced confusingly:

I saw a man chasing a cat with a broom in his underpants. Who has the broom? Where is it? How would you clarify this sentence?

Hold the grenade in one hand, pull out the pin with the other, and throw it. What gets thrown, pin or grenade? What would happen if a recruit read the instructions and threw the wrong thing?

As a child, death was unreal. Is death being personified, or does the writer mean, "When I was a child, death seemed unreal"?

Armed with this information, it is important to understand. Who is armed? What is "it"? Who is supposed to understand?

They lined up some kegs ready to consume. Could these be eager, animated kegs, straight off the Disney lot?

He never was able to get close to his father because he drank so much. Who drinks too much, son or father?

He set out with an elephant gun, with no intention of killing one. Who has the intention? What may get killed?'

We can make an impact on AIDS by openly talking to your mate. If we all start talking openly to your lover, you could be in big trouble.

He revealed that he got AIDS on TV. What happened on TV, revelation or infection?

I hit a tree going fifty miles an hour. That tree must be a rootless wonder!

Now see how best you can fix this one:

We must defeat the challenge before it defeats us by being unhappy.

LS (Logical Subject)—Similar to XA and DP but characterized by a dropped logical subject, or doer of the action presented by the verb. Examples:

A college education on a résumé will have a better chance. What is going to have a better chance?

Refusing to help an alcoholic should never be denied. Who is doing the refusing? What is to be denied?

Personally, the word itself takes both definitions with a twist. Here, *the word* is doing the taking, and the subject referred to by "personally" is nowhere in sight.

He trails the beast with a weapon. Who has the weapon?

Shame targets human nature to avoid feeling disgraced. Who is doing what, with which, and to whom?

Without anything to look forward to, life does not have any meaning. Whose life? Who is doing the "looking forward"?

Now try working on these two:

1. *Like many parents, a situation like Tom's would be agreed that it is too difficult.*
2. *Alcoholism doesn't have any set number of drinks which define the alcoholic.*

DO (Dropped Object)—A comparatively rare difficulty in which the receiver of the action being referred to by the verb is missing:

AIDS is a deadly, highly emotional, and controversial. The writer obviously meant to conclude with *disease* but in haste forgot. (Dropping the *a* and prefacing AIDS with *The subject of* is another possible remedy.)

Try creating a few examples for yourself.

NS (Non Sequitur—"it does not follow")—This can range from the blatant to the subtle but always involves saying something that does not logically follow what has been said before it:

They put their health at risk by destroying brain cells which cause cancer. Destroying brain cells does not necessarily impair health, though it can impair brain function; and the line ends with a causal fallacy which claims that brain cells cause cancer. If they do, then health would be improved, not placed at risk.

Since AIDS attacked without warning, doctors have not yet found a cure. The fact that researchers have not yet found a cure for AIDS does not follow from the unexpected emergence of the disease.

If they cannot develop independence, they will be unable to live with lovers. Being unable to live with a lover does not follow from individual inability to become independent.

Now rewrite these sentences to eliminate the non sequitur:

Shame comes hand-in-hand with self-respect.

Down's syndrome was as popular as mongolism.

CF (Causal Fallacy)—While this can be similar to the non sequitur, it specifically ascribes a result to the wrong or an unrelated cause. Examples:

They would be frightened because I don't think they know. Whatever these people don't know isn't clearly the cause of their fear.

Shame was being in over my head. How does shame relate to being in over one's head?

Writing because you don't feel good at it. What is the CF here? and how would you correct it?

ND (Not Demonstrated)—Unlike the non sequitur and the causal fallacy, ND identifies a statement that may be valid but remains not clearly demonstrated. Examples:

Love is not a feeling, it is a decision. Until the writer can demonstrate the claim that love is a decision, most of us would disagree and might scoff at the statement, since in our experience love definitely involves feelings, whereas a relationship involves decisions.

Shame is embodied in the human gene. Today, it appears to have become fashionable to blame everything on genetics, but unless the writer can demonstrate the claim, it remains an idle assertion.

As an exercise, try demonstrating this claim in as many ways as you can:

There are no bad words.

FC (False Conclusion)—In this, the writer makes a good observation, but then reaches a wrong, sometimes unrelated conclusion:

My friends were out when I called, so they must not like me anymore.

People wear bathing suits, which puts the beach in danger of being polluted.

Avocados are used in salads, which makes them a natural aphrodisiac.

Birds fly south in fall, and this brings winter.

Now try creating a few examples of your own, drawing on personal observations that might be used to reach wrong conclusions.

DN (Double Negative)—In some languages, double negatives may be used for emphasis. In English, however, two negatives make a positive, invalidating what the writer means:

I don't think I wouldn't visit. If you don't think that you wouldn't, then perhaps you do think that you would.

None of my brothers never had a chance. None never having a chance means that all of them did have a chance.

I'll do it only if I don't have to hurt nobody. Not hurting nobody does not preclude the possibility of hurting somebody.

SP (Singular/Plural)—In our age of inclusive language, SP has become one of the most insidious problems for the writer, affecting everyone from politicians to preachers, feminists to chauvinists. The scramble to eliminate presumed verbal sexism has left even scholars falling over themselves in an effort to avoid saying "The child . . . he" or "The child . . . he/she." This has led to a chaos of singular/plural confusion. To wit:

A child may tend to hide their feelings. How does one child get to be several?

One must look at what they have in their own life. Here we have one person turning into several, who then have only one life between them.

If a girl was too muscular, they might be considered a man. Since the line is obviously in reference to a woman, it would not be sexist to say, "If she were too muscular, she might be considered a man."

Everyone has their own style. Better wording might be, "Everyone has his or her own style" or "People have their own styles."

One can't blame their luck on others. "One can't blame one's luck . . ." "You can't blame your luck . . ." and "We can't blame our luck . . ." all avoid the *his/her* that the writer tried get around by using *their.*

Each differed with their own troubles. Again, *their* is intended to replace *his/her*, but it would be better to replace *each* with *they*, although the line itself is lackluster and needs to be reworked.

When a person was saved, they saw the light. The plural is used to avoid saying *he or she,* but it is simpler to say, "When people were . . . they," or "When you were . . . you."

Everyone faces a challenge in their life. We all face challenges in our lives, but just putting a period after *challenge* and cutting *in their life* acomplishes the same thing with fewer words.

Now correct the SP in this sentence:

A person can respect their self.

CS (Comma Splice)—This involves stitching two sentences together with a comma instead of separating them with a period, semicolon, dash, or sometimes a conjunction. In the following sentences, decide what you would do to remedy the CS, then rewrite and improve the sentence:

I have had to overcome fears, some were overcome with positive results.

Models are lean, rarely do you see a fat model.

She enjoys sports, volleyball is her favorite.

The move was coming, my parents talked about it.

I went to say hello, they ignored me.

I attended private school, it was a Christian school.

RO (Run-On)—Here, one sentence simply runs onto another because the needed punctuation has been omitted—usually in haste. How would you improve and eliminate the RO in the following?

They were nice people my mother went home.

I was never wild my parents thought me safe.

It was the center of her life everything revolved around it.

None of this helped it destroyed her self-image.

He started staying over this is a perfect example.

I was in the hot seat all eyes were on me.

We talk price some cringe a little.

SV (Subject/Verb)—When this problem occurs, we find a sentence in which the subject, verb, and object are present, but the subject doesn't work with the verb, or vice versa:

This must be the first subject to understand in helping to educate the people. The subject doesn't do the understanding, but possibly people do.

Living together has expanded within family members. What does the writer mean? that living together has grown in size? or that the practice of cohabitation without marriage is more common among people from the same family group?

Other situations go through similar predicaments. How can situations go? Or does the writer mean "People in other situations . . . "?

The mangled body pressed into the earth. This must be quite a corpse—unless we insert *was* before *pressed.*

See what you can do to correct SV in these two sentences:

> *Such an idea is entitled to everyone's own opinion.*
>
> *Shame is someone who knows the wrongdoing.*

AW (Another Word)—This means *pick* another word (underlined). You do the picking:

> *It can be transmitted through blood <u>transplants</u>.*
>
> *The family lives <u>in</u> our fish pond.*
>
> *Marriage is a sacred <u>vowel</u>.*
>
> *It <u>permits</u> them from getting married.*
>
> *The capacity of feeling shame is as <u>fundamental</u> as hands.*
>
> *I was a seventeen-year-old <u>hormone</u>.*
>
> *I <u>jungled</u> these things.*
>
> *It was an <u>earmark</u> in history.*

Dict (Dictionary . . . and closely related to AW)—Check underlined words in both your dictionary and thesaurus, tools that the winning writer uses frequently. Replace each of the underlined words with the correct one, rewriting the sentence where necessary:

> *She was younger than her <u>pears</u>.*
>
> *They are <u>conflicted</u>.*
>
> *They have a vast <u>spread</u> of knowledge.*

She was <u>boulimic</u> and drank alcohol.

It was a <u>headual</u> matter.

They had a lot of <u>biasness</u>.

Unprotected sex can result in the <u>conception</u> of AIDS.

There were <u>acceptions</u> to the rule.

Problems <u>continuely</u> came because the people were <u>conceded</u>.

She knew what she was <u>participating</u>.

They should put the condom on with a <u>bacteria</u>.

Accept the <u>factitious</u> people.

He was <u>nebulas</u> about what to do.

Mng? (Meaning?)—To have a line flagged "Mng?"—as could some of the sentences under Dict—indicates that the meaning is so unclear that there is no way to make a helpful suggestion. If you can even begin to understand what is meant in each of the following, try coming up with a clear version:

Self-respect is when someone is acted out.

They live at a lower rate of living.

The idea of purpose became the ideology for clothes.

I had to do drastic measures to accommodate people.

The verity of influence was great.

It enhances the life that is blunt.

His challenge indication of fear did not sink in.

He was pressured by the bulging focals of the evidence.

Frag (Fragmented or fractured sentence)—Broken sentences can be used for emphasis, and the effective ones are often exclamatory—"Quite a startling revelation!" When the thought, intention, or meaning is also incomplete, however, the fragmented idea needs to be completed. How would you complete the following?

As if nothing out of the ordinary took place.

Especially being that he is retarded.

A part of her life in which stereotypes were pushed.

From the president to the homeless.

Even though he had not seen the light.

Which I didn't used to mind.

No style of their own.

So they would be clean to wear.

The catch being no money.

Reph (Rephrase)—Sometimes a good thought needs rephrasing to put the idea across more effectively. To get a firm grasp of what this involves, rewrite the following:

Educating and acting by the resource, the people, is the only true chance of survival of this nation.

She defines shame as an appearance situation.

I could not provide a constant balance of my cash drawer.

Young people will go against values their parents have taught them to engage in irresponsibility.

They put up barriers of cliques.

I have always relished the acquisition of the knowledge of many various things.

In relation, I will present my challenge which encompassed me being saved by God.

Tns (Tense)—Although shifting tense can sometimes be effective, usually it is far better to stay with the same tense throughout: past, present, future. Problems tend to occur when a writer begins with one tense and after awhile forgetfully shifts to another, but occasionally the shift may be made from one sentence to another, which can lead us to wonder when the action is occurring:

She is obsessed. She tried everything.

He was not alone. He feels good.

AV (Use Active Voice)—Unless you are in a delicate situation that requires tact and diplomacy, it is almost always better to say "I did it" (active voice) than "It was done by me" (passive voice). Give or take credit for an action or thought where credit is due. Failure to do so is not only a bit blah, it can lead to dropping the logical subject. Examples:

Love was not shown. By whom?

Speaking to someone would come to mind. Whose mind?

This will be proved in the comparison of apples and oranges. I will prove this by comparing apples and oranges.

There were many feelings I had. I had a lot of feelings.

There was no idea in the minds of his parents. His parents had no idea.

A sense of paranoia set in. Into whom?

This was contended by the witness. The witness contended . . .

A reason for living would not exist. I would lose reason to live.

My anger was brought by them. They made me angry.

While this concludes "Alphabet Soup," there are a number of miscellaneous items that we need to bear in mind:

Catch-alls—These include the words *very, really, somewhat, virtual,* and other vague modifiers which get thrown in because it takes work to replace them with something specific (the specific in turn being vulnerable to challenge). But what do we mean when we say that something was *very nice, really good, somewhat boring,* or *virtually true*?

That/who—It has become frustratingly commonplace to hear people say things like "my friends that . . . ," or "the parents that . . . ." *Who* is the relative pronoun for humans, and *that* is the relative pronoun for things. To use them interchangeably can result in confusion when you have both a thing and an individual as antecedents. Is it "the doctor in the hospital that treated cancer," meaning that it was a cancer hospital, or "the doctor in the hospital who treated cancer," meaning that the doctor was an oncologist?

Person(s)—In the effort to desex English by changing words like *chairman* to *chairperson,* many writers (and speakers) seem to have embraced the security of overusing *person,* giving us such awkward combinations as *waitperson* and *henchperson.* They forget that the *son* in *person* is also male and thus needs to be dropped as well for consistency. A logical extension of this "correctness" would change *human* to *huperson,* then *huper,* *woman* to *woperson*, then *woper*. The whole point of the winning writer's communication is to be fair, regardless of gender, not engage in linguistic contortions.

Collective nouns—Health and life apply to many people, but *health* is a collective noun, and *life* is not. That is, we can say *our health* and *their health*, but not *our life* and *their life*. *Life* is a singular, not a collective, noun, and *lives* is its plural.

Split infinitives—It has long been considered the hallmark of impeccable grammar never to split an infinitive. Putting that another way, "to never split" an infinitive is considered incorrect. But sometimes splitting is more effective than not splitting. A notable example is *Star Trek's* "To boldly go"—certainly stronger than "to go boldly." To split or not to split—the choice is yours. Make it wisely.

Concluding prepositions—Ending a sentence in a preposition—*in, on, by, to,* etc.—has long been considered as incorrect as splitting an infinitive. But, "What are you counting on?" is much stronger than "On what are you counting?" The same goes for "That is the house I live in," as opposed to "That is the house in which I live." Rules are good. They are also meant, on occasion, to be prudently broken.

Look-alike, sound-alike words—These are words that are frequently misused because they either sound or look the same. Make a note of them. And here is a preliminary list to which you can add (it's also a list you can add to):

peer	their	to	cite	soul	accept
pier	there	too	site	sole	except
pear	they're	two	sight		
bear	duel	alter	affect	then	
bare	dual	altar	effect	than	
ensure	whose	advice	course	your	
insure	who's	advise	coarse	you're	
loose	choose	brassiere	piece	complement	
lose	chose	brazier	peace	compliment	
week	whole	lessen	right	bean	
weak	hole	lesson	rite	been	

The contraction *could've* has also led to the sound-alike misuse, *could of.*

Euphemisms, jargon, and clichés—A euphemism can be a kind way of saying something—calling a person a "senior citizen" instead of "old," "hard of hearing" instead of "deaf." But the practice of avoiding the blunt truth can also be misleading. Why say "broken home" instead of "divorced"? "powder room" instead of "toilet"? "drinking problem" instead of "drunk"? "falling out" instead of "fight"? "a little short" instead of "broke"?

Jargon is another form of verbal evasiveness, whereby institutional gobbledegook is deployed to obscure what is happening. Thus, a "predawn vertical insertion" doesn't refer to early-morning sexual activity but to "an 0500 attack by helicopter," and "servicing the target" has nothing to do with cleaning or replacing targets, it means "shoot the man."

Clichés, on the other hand, aren't intended to obscure, but they do anyway. What, after all, is the "light at the end of the tunnel"—a way out? or just another train? What is "not my cup of tea"—something you don't like, or someone else's cup? And what is "the bottom line"—the actual cost or meaning, or the lowest in a series of lines?

To be as clear as possible implies reverence for the truth.

Vary—When sentences all plod along using the same structure, you need to see how you can vary them to avoid monotony. The basic components of the sentence are subject, verb, and object. Simple sentences include little else: *We played ball. They ate cake. Jill kissed Jack.* But these can be varied in many ways. To explore how, let's work with the following:

The students prepared for the test.

The simplest step in changing a sentence is to add modifiers—adjectives to qualify nouns, adverbs to complement verbs:

The new students diligently prepared for the difficult test.

Since everything added to a sentence provides more information, the reader now knows that while these are not experienced students, they are prepared to work hard in the face of challenge. We assume them to be academic. But what happens if we add two words:

The new students diligently prepared for the difficult test of endurance.

This casts an entirely new light on the sentence and leads us to the next step in development: making the sentence a compound one. That is, we will use a conjunction to add another clause:

The new students diligently prepared for the difficult test of endurance, <u>and they did so at the gymnasium</u>.

Of course, this added clause can also be modified:

and they did so <u>quietly</u> at the <u>military</u> gymnasium.

Now we have given the reader even more information and might consider adding a subordinate clause:

The new students diligently prepared for the difficult test of endurance, and they did so quietly at the military gymnasium, <u>though no one seemed to notice</u>.

Although this is already a cumbersome sentence, let's try encumbering it a bit more by fronting the line, breaking into it, and adding an overloaded conclusion:

<u>Gathered in twos and threes, their faces wan in the gloomy light,</u> the new students—<u>five hundred of them, their numbers growing by the minute</u>—diligently prepared for the difficult test of endurance, and they did so quietly at the military gymnasium, though no one seemed to notice, <u>despite chanting by Tibetan monks in black and weeping by vestal virgins in white</u>.

Obviously, such a sentence is not one to brag about, but it does give you an idea of how you can vary your own sentences and have a good time while you do so.

Enjoy!

Digging In—
Another Appendix

At one point or another, almost everyone has faced the prospect of taking an essay exam, with little or no time to prepare amid rampant distractions. While none of us welcomes such experiences, the winning writer at least tries to set aside negative energy and look to what can be done using available resources, including the proverbial "shovel"—a tool commonly frowned upon by those who pretend they never use it.

To cite a personal example of shovelmanship, I became a father early one morning during finals week in my junior year at Yale. I spent all night at the hospital, alternately attending to my wife and trying to cram, my textbooks spread out on the floor. Finally the baby arrived, and after I had assured myself that mother and son were O.K., I ran across New Haven to take an 8:00 A.M. sociology final. When I arrived, feeling like a hip pocket turned inside out, everyone was already bent over bluebooks, and I sat down breathlessly to look at the two-hour essay question:

Discuss the impact on American immigration of the 1850 Irish Potato Famine.

And I said to myself, "Irish Potato *what!?*"

Faced with a major call for creative use of the shovel (either that or just sit there and fail), I dug in, employing a method that follows the basic lines of organizing thoughts for an article or for a term paper. Here are the steps I went through to write well—and authoritatively—enough to score an honors grade on something I knew little about. The italics indicate areas of shovel activity.

1.   For there to be a famine, potatoes must have been the staple crop of Ireland. *(Discuss the social history of Ireland, the suitability of its environment for growing potatoes, opportunistic diseases that could destroy crops, and the time lag between onset of crop loss and onset of critical hunger problems. Mention famine data gathered from India and Africa.)*

2.   Since primogeniture was the law of the land, the eldest son was in luck, but daughters and all other sons were not. *(Explain the economic reasons for primogeniture as a way of keeping land from being cut into increasingly small parcels, and its particular impact on Ireland's large Catholic families. Also discuss the social, emotional, and religious implications of leaving everything to the first son; refer briefly to my new son, as well as to my own first-son standing.)*

3.   The have-nots would probably then take whatever boats they could find and make the hazardous Atlantic crossing from Ireland to the nearest port in America: Boston, where only bluebloods lived, moved, and had their beans. *(Review the social, cultural, historical, literary, and political importance of the clam chowder capital of the world as the major eastern seaboard city of the period, replete with Yankee Clippers and missionary zeal. Touch upon Mayflower elitism.)*

4.   At the time, Boston was populated largely by genteel Protestants, who would not take kindly to threadbare, rawboned Catholic boat people willing to work for next to nothing, possibly lowering the standard of living, affecting politics and the balance of power. *(Examine reasons why the Protestants who had first fled from England, seeking religious freedom, might feel threatened by and therefore prejudiced against the Catholic newcomers seeking economic freedom. Also note that while the language of friendship evolves, the language of prejudice never changes. Use current bigoted statements against minorities as 1850 quotes to illustrate what Boston newspapers said about the Irish.)*

5.   The Protestants would then write angry letters to their elected representatives in Washington. *(Key in on the social force of letter writing and pamphleteering, their role in the independence movement, the power of the written word.)*

6.   In the 1800s, Massachusetts was a political stronghold, and its representatives could probably succeed in establishing immigration quotas. Such quotas would then remain in force until repealed, creating difficulties for new immigrants. Added restraints would make it impossible for Irish families to rise, socially or economically, until Joe Kennedy

struck it rich in bootleg. *(For a thematic conclusion, tie back to potatoes, and their use in making bootleg, briefly turning the closing line on the Irish rise from potato famines to potato fortunes.)*

I am still not sure how much of this can be substantiated, but, entertaining though it may be, and despite a satisfactorily disarming spirit of self-confidence, you are of course far better off if you have had adequate time to prepare. Here are the five steps that will help you win on essay exams:

1. Take clear, effective notes at every class. Record your reactions.
2. Take notes on all reading assignments, and highlight the text(s).
3. Before the exam, review your notes at least three times.
4. Pick a study partner, and ask each other questions related to the course.
5. Review your notes again, and again, and . . .

Also, if in your writing program you are accustomed to critiquing each other in class (this is called workshopping), your experience with the following format will be an added benefit to you:

Workshop Format

Outlining

Thesis: Statement of message, with an edge of vulnerability

Plan: Clear indication of how the thesis will be supported

Support: Full development of main supporting examples

Conclusion: Effective closing paragraph on the significance of your thesis

Using these four points, outline your essay and list anything that you think might improve it in revision.

Evaluating

A. Pair off and exchange papers. Read your partner's paper and outline it, in your *own* words writing down what you think are the thesis, plan, support, and conclusion. Then write your answers to the following six questions:

1. How could the thesis be made stronger and clearer?
2. What could be done to improve support?
3. Where could the plan be changed to smooth transitions?
4. How can the conclusion be made more effective?
5. What is the paper's weakest point?
6. What is its strongest point?

Recheck your answers, adding any information that you think might be helpful to your partner. Give your critique to him or her after discussing your views, and write your name—as well as your partner's—on the page for identification at any subsequent sessions.

B. Now, on a separate page, list five things that you think your partner could do to improve his or her paper in revision, and five things that you think you can do to improve *your* paper. Share this information with your partner.

C. Change partners, and critique your new partner, using the same steps.

This basic format can be extremely useful as you develop the habit of outlining what you plan to say before you start to write.

But practice with the format can also be helpful when you work on a term paper. Since my undergraduate days, such assignments have become increasingly sophisticated, and could in some cases pass for article proposals. Consider the following examples. The first I assigned to an English 301 class (Writing for the Professions), the second to English 105 (Basic Composition):

A. Select a professional field in which you are keenly interested, or plan to enter, and identify what you consider to be its major ethical problem. Research this problem in depth, and write a 5,000-word investigative report, using case histories to demonstrate your thesis, and generating concluding ideas about workable solutions to the problem.

B. Compare the similarities in and differences between relationships that succeed and those that fail. Drawing on examples from literature, the news, documentaries, and people you know, write a 2,500-word paper that presents ways to improve survival rates and minimize failure rates.

In **A**, before you can come up with a dynamic thesis and plan, you need to research the field that you've chosen. Let's say that you selected engineering because you are majoring in it. Your first recourse is a professor in the department of engineering. He or she may offer you a few key suggestions. Follow up on them. At the same time, and throughout the project, you should be researching your library's files of newspapers, magazines, and journals, calling on advice from the librarian as you use the computer system to track out new leads. Also, you might arrange to interview a few engineers.

Somewhere during this process, which will generate force as you pursue it, a strong thesis will emerge or suddenly occur to you. It may, of course, change as your research expands, but let's say that what has you excited is this: *The major ethical problem in engineering is corporate pressure to maximize profits by compromising test data in order to sell or field something before it is demonstrably safe to use.* (You might also note that greed—for money or for power—gives rise to ethical problems in most fields, from medicine to sports, from politics to finance.) At this point, you are ready to look for strong supporting examples in the automotive and aerospace industries, manufacturers of military equipment, NASA, construction, and so forth. And don't cross off any parallel examples that you might happen upon in communications, entertainment, and finance. For instance, the motion picture *Class Action,* starring Gene Hackman, might give you some good ideas. Each illustration that you select then needs to be carefully researched. As you develop your argument, your conclusion will become apparent—possibly, say, that the best way to offset the corrosive influence of greed is not to incarcerate but to impoverish the scoundrels.

The result of hard, caring, and thoughtful work is usually good grades. More important, the winning writer grows in the process, may even wind up with a publishable term paper.

As for **B**, you need to follow much the same process; but in this case you have more leeway to review novels, short stories, journals, news reports, movies, and docudramas. You can also interview your parents, friends, and teachers. Again, consider the library your great resource, the librarian your strong ally—as well as your potential review*ee.*

In time, your thesis will grow from your information-gathering efforts. Let's say you suddenly realize that in enduring relationships, the partners look to what they can *give* each other; that in relationships that fail, the partners look only to what they can *get* from each other. At this point, you have a wonderful opportunity to pick at least two of the most moving positive examples and at least two of the most moving negative examples, then examine remarriages to reach your conclusion that when people embrace the creative, generous power of love, they embrace the power to change, to make life whole, to find what they seek.

One final point. When I first started writing, I hand-wrote (which is still the case with in-class essay exams), then copied the draft on the typewriter. Every time I revised the manuscript, I would have to *re*type it. When word-processing computers first became available as a writer's option, the executive editor of a national book club warned me not to use one; he said that when you got frustrated with typewritten text, you might crumple the page and throw it on the floor, but you could always retrieve it to salvage what you liked. Hitting the "delete" key on the computer, on the other hand, erased everything permanently—which of course is not so, though it wasn't until I taught a CompuWrite course at Cal State Polytechnic University in Pomona that I became aware of the inaccuracy of such advice. While I would just as soon not have computers (or, for that matter, typewriters) in a writing classroom, where the need is to exchange ideas, discuss literature, not work with a machine, I cannot possibly overstate what a great asset you will find the computer to be in your writing. Indeed, software now available offers modes of note taking and outlining that enhance the ease with which you can arrive at an excellent final draft of whatever project you are working on. With access to a printer, a scanner, a modem, and the Internet, you will find that the exchange of information strengthens your research, your digging in, your intellectual development of creative ideas on which the future of our world depends.

For starters, transfer **Workshop Format** to a floppy disc, and on your next project try writing notes under the headings "Thesis," "Plan," "Support," and "Conclusion."

Reader List

Suggested stories and articles for a separate

reader to accompany The Winning Writer

Ten of the Best Short Stories

Faulkner, William. "Dry September," *Collected Stories of Faulkner.*
Fitzgerald, F. Scott. "Babylon Revisited," *The Stories of Fitzgerald.*
Hemingway, Ernest. "The Short Happy Life of Francis Macomber," *The Short Stories of Hemingway.*
Hemingway, Ernest. "The Snows of Kilimanjaro," *The Short Stories of Hemingway.*
Miller, Arthur. "Mount St. Angelo," *Stories of Sudden Truth.*
O'Connor, Frank. "Guests of the Nation," *More Stories by O'Connor.*
Salinger, J.D. "For Esmé—With Love and Squalor," *Nine Stories by Salinger.*
Thurber, James. "The Secret Life of Walter Mitty, *New Yorker Stories.*
White, Robin. "First Voice," *Best American Short Stories 1958.*
White, Robin. "Shower of Ashes," *O. Henry Prize Stories 1960.*

Ten Top Articles . . . plus one

Ackerman, Diane. "Taste," *A Natural History of the Senses,* 1991.
Bird, Caroline. "College Is a Waste of Time and Money," *The Case against College,* 1975.
Calendra, Alexander. "Angels on a Pin," *Saturday Review,* December 26, 1968.
Chisholm, Shirley. "Outlawing Compulsory Pregnancy Laws," *Abortion Rap,* 1971.
Hick, John. "The Problem of Evil," *Philosophy of Religion,* 1973.
Jacoby, Susan. *Unfair Game,* 1978.
Lurie, Alison. *The Language of Clothes,* 1981.
Montague, Louise. "Straight Talk about the Living-Together Arrangement," *Reader's Digest,* April 1977.
Rachels, James. "Active and Passive Euthanasia," *New England Journal of Medicine,* Vol. 290, 1975, pp. 78–80.
White, Robin. "The Battle for Understanding," *Saturday Evening Post,* January 1961.
White, Robin, and White, Marny. "The Egyptian Identity of Moses," *Imprint of Stanford Libraries,* Vol. 7, No. 2, October 1981.

Index

Acknowledgments

Robin White, "The Choice." From *Why Work?* Copyright © 1965 by BRL, Menlo Park, California. Reprinted by permission of the author.

Robin White, "The Forgotten Minority." Published in Scripps-Howard newspapers, 1984. Reprinted by permission of the author.

Robin White, "Backpacker Sketches," Vol. 3, No. 2, p. 27. Copyright © 1968 by *Per/Se* Magazine. Copyright renewed 1996. Reprinted by permission of the author.

Robin White, *Be Not Afraid,* pp. 115–116. Copyright © 1971 by Robin White. Reprinted by permission of the author.

Bret Sporich, "News Story." From Pasadena *Star-News,* p. B3, January 27, 1994. Copyright © 1994 by Thomson L.A. News Group. Reprinted by permission of the editors.

Kenneth Turan, "Review." From *The Los Angeles Times,* p. F1, February 4, 1994. Copyright © 1994 by The Times-Mirror Company. Reprinted by permission of the editors.

Ron Tepper, *Power Resumes,* p. 48. Copyright © 1989 by John Wiley & Sons. Reprinted by permission of the publisher.

Excerpt from *Black Boy* by Richard Wright, pp. 284–285. Copyright © 1937, 1942, 1944, 1945 by Richard Wright. Copyright renewed 1973 by Ellen Wright. Reprinted by permission of HarperCollins Publishers, Inc.

Page 1 from *The Hero Within* by Carol S. Pearson. Copyright © 1987 by Carol S. Pearson. Reprinted by permission of HarperCollins Publishers, Inc.